# MOTHERPRAYER

# MOTHERPRAYER

THE PREGNANT WOMAN'S
SPIRITUAL COMPANION

Tikva Frymer-Kensky

RIVERHEAD BOOKS
NEW YORK
1995

*Sefer Raziel* (Amsterdam, 1701), folios 43a and b, reprinted courtesy of the Library of the Jewish Theological Seminary of America.

Riverhead Books
a division of G. P. Putnam's Sons
*Publishers Since 1838*
200 Madison Avenue
New York, NY 10016

Library of Congress Cataloging-in-Publication Data

Frymer-Kensky, Tikva Simone.
Motherprayer : the pregnant woman's spiritual
companion / by Tikva Frymer-Kensky.
p.    cm.
ISBN 1-57322-011-6 (alk. paper)
1. Pregnant women—Prayer-books and devotions—
English.   2. Jewish women—Prayer-books and devotions
—English.   3. Christian women—Prayer-books and
devotions—English.   4. Judaism—Prayer-books and
devotions—English.   5. Childbirth—Religious aspects—
Judaism—Meditations.   6. Childbirth—Religious aspects—
Christianity—Meditations.   7. Pregnancy—Religious
aspects—Judaism—Meditations.   8. Pregnancy—Religious
aspects—Christianity—Meditations.   I. Title.
BM667.W6F78   1995
296.7'2—dc20                                95-20333 CIP

Printed in the United States of America
1   3   5   7   9   10   8   6   4   2

*Book design by Judith Stagnitto Abbate*

This book is printed on acid-free paper. ∞

*For my mother, Elyse Hirshberg Frymer,
and my daughter, Meira Ziva Frymer Kensky,
and for all mothers and daughters everywhere.*

# CONTENTS

# INTRODUCTION

$M$otherprayer is the result of a seventeen-year investigation into the Jewish and Christian traditions relating to pregnancy and childbirth. At the same time, most of the readings and poems in *Motherprayer* are my own original compositions. In these two apparently contradictory sentences lies a silence. It is the story of this book.

Seventeen years ago, when I was pregnant with my daughter, Meira, professional academic women were expected to ignore their pregnancies, concentrate on their work, have their babies casually, and then return to work two weeks later as if nothing more momentous had taken place than a trip to Chicago. My Lamaze class was the one hour a week when I was permitted to talk about being pregnant. About the thirty-eighth week I began to sense that something was wrong. I knew that the baby's head was supposed to engage in my pelvis, but I kept feeling a bouncing back and forth as if the head were hitting something. I told my doctor, and in the fortieth week he ordered an X-ray. He called me in to see it, and told me that we couldn't risk labor: that my spine was sticking out into the birth canal (the result of a back trauma more than a decade earlier) and that the baby might crush her skull against my spine. He then gave me one hour to go home, pack my bags, and get back to the hospital so that I could be prepared for a Cesarean section early the next morning.

I drove home distraught and quickly got things ready. I knew that my husband would leave for evening services at seven o'clock and that I would face a long, anxious evening alone. I took the two novels that I had put aside for after the birth, the TV guide so that I could lose myself in television and, by an act of divine Providence or sheer lunacy, a file folder full of Sumerian and Akkadian birth incantations. I didn't have these texts for any birth-related reason: I had just finished a massive study of the judicial ordeal in the ancient world which included, for various reasons, an analysis of the significance of water in Mesopotamian religion. The birth incantations, many of which had been published by a Sumerologist I had studied with in Rome, had a lot of water symbolism, and so the file folder sat innocently in my file cabinet until the night before my daughter's birth.

At the hospital that evening, after my husband had left, I couldn't read the novels. Nor did I want to watch TV. In fact, I did not want to distract or transport myself at all. On the contrary, I wanted to focus my thoughts on what was going to happen, to direct my attention to childbirth and the experience of it. And so I spent a long evening happily studying these ancient birth incantations. As I read them, I felt the tradition of millennia of women who had given birth before me. I felt their strain and their joy and felt connected to the great cosmic process of renewal. My fears and anxieties about childbirth ceased to be the private emotions of an isolated woman and became, instead, a part of the grand challenge of human endeavors. My own short life span became extended by a spiritual communion with women past and future. I became conscious of the magnitude of birth; I grew spiritually tranquil and ready to marshall my will.

Later, after I had fully recovered from the birth and the general anaesthesia—around ten and a half months later—I began to get angry. Why was it, I wanted to know, that I, well educated in Judaism and in Christianity, had to go all the way back to ancient Babylon in order to find something to read before childbirth? And what could most women do, who do not read Sumerian?

I spent the next two years finding out the answers to these questions. In 1978, the answers were not as well known as they may seem today. I read the new feminist literature that was emerging, and in particular studies of women and religion. After a few years of studying and teaching about women and religion, I began to understand the factors that had contributed to the lack of childbirth literature. First, most literature has been written largely by men and for men. Even when we know that women wrote, their writings have not generally been preserved. Second, Western thought has often seen the world in pairs of polar opposites: good/evil, up/down, right/left, male/female, human/animal, culture/nature, mind/body. The body decays, the mind or spirit are deemed immortal and considered to hold the true life. Our religious communities have a difficult relationship with the body and do not celebrate biological life processes as occasions for spiritual growth and communication with the divine. Menstruation, sexual initiation, climacteric and menopause are met with tabooed silence. We even take the body out of puberty, marking a child's coming-of-age with celebration of brain and skill—and ignoring the sexual and emotional changes of adolescence.

We have ignored or sought to control and repress everything that makes women female, and everything that makes men *male*. There are no traditional religious texts that explore men's relations to their penis, that express the competing emotions that arousal may bring, or describe a sacred understanding of the powerful feeling of orgasm. There are no rituals or

xiv    M O T H E R P R A Y E R

prayers that refer to a young man's first ejaculation, or an older man's first experience of impotence, or the return of potency after impotence. There is no language to understand spiritually the awesome markers of growing up. There are also no texts that confront the social and emotional facets of being a man: the birth of a child, the responsibilities and feelings of fatherhood, the act of marriage, separation, reconciliation, divorce, retirement.

Ignoring the body is particularly alienating for women. Much of our lives are and have always been spent in relation to our bodies. We have always had to coordinate our social roles with menstruation and menopause, pregnancy and nursing. At the same time, cultural prejudices against women and social taboos about menstruating and pregnant women have often kept women away from society's communal, social, and intellectual interactions. Our religions have often distanced themselves from our body activities and have kept us distant from the activities that they value.

Modern secular Western society has just as many problems with the body. Our culture does not denigrate the body —as long as it is youthful, muscled and lean, with flat abdomen, steely buttocks, and articulated pectorals. Women have to be hardbodies while staying "feminine"—not too broad backed or heavy muscled. The fat, decrepit, or aging body is often a cause for derision or, at the very least, pity. We treat bodily infirmity and illness as failure, prolong life past dignity, starve ourselves, induce vomiting, and abuse our bodies with many harmful and addictive substances.

At first sight it might seem that childbirth has been the one physical event to which Western traditions have paid attention. Birth, after all, is an important event in the life of a community, for without births, communities die out, as have the Shakers and other celibate communities. Judaism and Christianity are markedly pronatal, desiring and encouraging procreation. They celebrate childbirth with infant namings, baptisms, and circumcisions. But the focus of these religious celebrations is on the child; our religions have paid little attention to the mother, assuming that childbirth was woman's allotted role and that her biology was her destiny. The process of pregnancy itself, with its fears, anxieties, joys, and perils, has been largely ignored. In the Christian world, women were even confined once their pregnancy began to "show" for fear that the sight of a pregnant women would cause people to think about how she got that way.

Once I had understood these issues, my anger at the silence surrounding childbirth dissipated. I realized that my years of academic study of the ancient world could have practical applications and my knowledge of ancient cultures, religions, and languages could be of use in my own modern world. I was seized with a sense of mission, to start to fill the silence that I had heard so clearly the night before my daughter's birth. This sense of vocation has sustained me in the many years that I have been working on this book.

I began very innocently. When I suddenly became aware of the profound silence of our religious traditions regarding the spiritual dimensions of pregnancy and childbirth, the void and the imperative to fill it both seemed obvious. After all, there were millions of women who, like me, were active members of their faith communities. Among these were many educated women who had at least begun to develop a feminist consciousness. Many of these women had been or would be pregnant and bear children. It seemed absolutely self-evident to me that the religious traditions in which these women were active should also begin to address issues and experiences that belonged primarily to women. I wanted our religions to pay attention to pregnancy, and I would try to find a means to expand our religious traditions in ways that were still faithful to them.

I began and completed this book blissfully unaware that this project that seemed to me, an American Feminist Jew, imperative and uncomplicated, rests on principles that are axiomatic to me but may be contested by others. The first principle is the assumption that having children is an important activity. It is not the easiest of enterprises, for it involves dedication and self-sacrifice, even during the months of pregnancy, and certainly for the rest of child rearing. It has also often been the occasion of much sorrow for women, often fatal, almost always painful, and sometimes ending with the tragedy of miscarriage, stillbirth, and perinatal death. Birth also *defined* women and limited their roles in society. Biology was destiny: women were expected to have children, women who did not give birth were considered "barren" and unfortunate, and a woman who did not want to have children was somehow unnatural, unwomanly, devoid of the "maternal instinct." Society had a vested interest in women's wombs and sought to guard them by excluding women from occupations that might endanger their reproductive powers.

Considering this cultural history, it is not surprising that one of feminism's first tasks was to break the link between biology and destiny and provide women with the freedom to say no to childbearing. Birth control and abortion provided the technological means to do so, but it was also necessary to expose and grapple with the cultural factors and assumptions that limited women's freedom to choose. There is a whole literature, beginning with Adrienne Rich's *Of Woman Born*, that analyzes the social implications of motherhood. There is another body of literature, deriving from Nancy Chodorow's *The Reproduction of Mothering*, that studies the various ways that women are influenced culturally to want to have children. These studies have been so influential that for a while childbearing seemed positively retrograde and unfeminist. Nevertheless, feminism's aim has always been to enlarge women's freedom of action, and the fact of the matter is that many women do wish to have children, for a whole variety of reasons. These women—I among them—do not thereby give up our desire to be considered adult, intelligent and spiritual beings, and have a right to have our choices validated and supported by other women and by our religious communities. This book is not written to convince women to have children; it is written to provide women who have chosen this path with religious imagery and language to maximize the spiritual dimensions of this choice.

The second principle on which this book is based is my firm commitment both to monotheism and to its feminist transformation. I look for my religious imagery and language in the texts of Judaism and Christianity, mining them to create the poems and meditations in this book. The androcentricity of these texts alienates many women and has angered some feminists to the point of rejection. These women look elsewhere for their spirituality, to traditions that they hope say something more positive about bodies, or to their own creativity, forming new rituals based on the lived experience of women. This is not my path: my own religious understanding and spiritual quest have been shaped by thousands of years of Jewish tradition, as well as by my own personal experiences and the events and learning of the modern world. I do not want to leave my own religious tradition in order to express my female-ness. I do not want to spend Sabbath at synagogue and give birth in a coven. To do so would re-create and perpetuate the old pernicious division between body and mind from which all of us have suffered for so long. There are many women like me who are Christians and Jews. The religious heritage of the West is our spiritual language. It provides our identity and tradition and gives us the communal symbols and idioms that enable us to communicate our spiritual experiences and to learn from each other and from the generations before us. This is the framework in which we find our spiritual inspiration. We cannot seek the spiritual significance of the female aspects of our lives without centering that search in our Judaeo-Christian heritage. We cannot nourish only our communal and intellectual selves in the church or synagogue and find meaning for our bodily selves elsewhere. We want to connect our cultural roots and our physical bodies and ground our spirituality in both our lived experiences and our religious texts.

When there is silence in the texts, we must act to fill that silence. We need to recover and transform our religious heritage to extend the images and concepts of our religions to incorporate our lives as individual embodied women. But our religious texts—androcentric and incomplete as they are—are the repositories of our cultural memory. They confront us with our past, and we cannot ignore them. If we hold on to them, they will change in our grasp, like Proteus, until eventually they tell us what we want to know. If we keep wrestling with the divine all night, as Jacob did, it will give us its blessing. This engagement with our past traditions keeps our religions alive and responsive to our new sensibility.

This is not a radical enterprise. Religions have always grown by an organic process of recombining and reinterpreting the religious past. But these changes have been very slow, and we have had little awareness that they were happening. Now that we have become aware of flaws and gaps, we must wrestle with the tradition in order to do the same thing in a more conscious way.

The third controversial principle on which this book is based is my belief that the renewal and transformation of religion in the twenty-first century involves a willingness to conduct the discourse throughout monotheism. As an American

Jew, I am deeply aware of Christian ideas. The culture in which I live and out of which I form my own spirituality is not only influenced by my Judaism: all of Western culture is my playground and my treasure house. Moreover, as monotheist faiths, Christianity and Judaism share monotheism's transcendent realization of the unity of creation and of divinity. Historical relations between these religious communities have been somewhat strained, to say the least. Christians have been hostile, intent on proving the Jewish texts wrong and the Christian texts right. Or they have been supercessionist, accepting the Jewish text as valuable and declaring that it no longer belonged to Jews but to Christians. Jews have responded defensively, drawing their boundaries very strongly and assuming that Christianity and Judaism never communicated with each other. The burden of this past history exacts a great price in fear and defensiveness, and is better laid aside. Judaism and Christianity are sister monotheist religions that have constantly learned from each other. They have much to say to each other in the contemporary universe.

Women have both an opportunity and an obligation to engage in this interfaith dialogue. The shared experiences of Western women, particularly those revolving around areas of the female body and childbirth, transcend the boundaries of faith and culture. Moreover, we are at the beginning of creating religious language and imagery for women's experiences. There is a vast silence and an opportunity for women to fill the silence, casting their spiritual net as widely as possible.

I am not advocating any merging of Judaism and Christianity into some sort of vague Judaeo-Christianism or lowest common denominator monotheism. On the contrary, I find our particular faith communities the repositories of vast and intricate spiritual and cultural traditions. The more we learn and invest in our own communities, the richer our cultural lives. But we must be able to define our identities and protect our communities without "otherizing" others. Religion and culture are not zero-sum gains, and the quality of divinity is infinite. Sharing religious insights can only enrich all of us.

There are so many forces in the contemporary world—economic and ecological, technological and cultural—that lead to the degradation of human life. And there are formidable "others" who are far more unlike us than we are unlike one another. These include new fundamentalisms that encourage people to give up their own ability and authority to develop in new ways, and a secularism that gives no spiritual direction at all in a very complicated universe. The sanctity of human life and its creation demands that we form a common language to talk about and work for its continued sanctification.

I began by reading the extant literature about the nonmedical aspects of childbirth. Since 1978 there has been an explosion of information. There are now many books on the mechanics, the psychology, the anthropology, and the politics of childbirth. For most women, the experience of delivery has changed from the passive Twilight Sleep experience of the 1950s to today's more participatory childbirth methods. Nevertheless, despite this growth of information about birthing, the many months of actual pregnancy have continued to be relegated to the medical domain and ignored from a spiritual perspective.

I wanted to find out where the silence manifested itself: What were the points and issues of pregnancy when women felt stress and sensed the absence of a symbolic language? I talked with other women and, in particular, with midwives. I discovered that pregnant women are often ill at ease about pain and discomfort; about the size and shape of pregnancy; about the practice of self-denial and the realization that this other-directedness is going to be characteristic of motherhood; about the anxieties and fears that they have for themselves and for the unborn child. These are the questions about which childbearing women feel the silence of our cultural traditions most acutely, and these are the issues that both call for and provide a spiritual framework for the pregnancy experience.

The process begins with a search for ancient references to childbirth. For this volume, I have translated texts from Sumerian, Akkadian, Hebrew, Yiddish, Old French and French, Latin, and Aramaic. These ancient texts are mostly concerned with the pain and dread of labor. They include magic texts, mostly inscribed on amulets, which could be worn or hung on the wall during times of stress and danger. Some of these amulets were to prevent miscarriage, others contain prayers for easy and safe deliveries, and still others seek to protect mother and child from the child-snatching demon. The ancient texts also contain prayers for the protection of woman and child. Prominent among these are three groups of ancient prayers from the sixteenth to the nineteenth centuries. One group, in French, has prayers to St. Marguerite, often considered the patron saint of childbirth. Her legend was recited and inscribed as an amulet, and special prayers were composed to her. Another group, in Hebrew, survives mostly in hand-copied prayer books for women crafted in eighteenth-century Italy. These are petitionary prayers addressed to God and, to a lesser extent, the angels, to be recited throughout pregnancy and childbirth. The third group, in Old Yiddish and Yiddish, are petitionary prayers, called *tekhines*, printed in special prayerbooks for women in central and eastern Europe. The two separate Jewish prayer traditions contain prayers that are literal translations from Hebrew to Yiddish or from Yiddish to Hebrew, or possibly even parallel translations of an original liturgical Aramaic.

In some cases, straight translation did not seem to be

enough. Many of these ancient texts, particular those of Mesopotamia, are full of the names of ancient gods and references
to ancient ideas familiar to only a small group of scholars in
the modern world. Nevertheless, the ideas that they contain
are poignant and stimulating. I have chosen to paraphrase
some of the Sumerian birth incantations in one poem ("sailing
to birth") and weave together several Akkadian childsnatcher
incantations into "The Daughter of An." The many birth incantations from Mesopotamiam, Byzantine Greek, Arabic, Hebrew and Aramaic and Persian that express the battle of the
saviors against the childsnatcher are paraphrased together in
"SSSS." The ancient incantations and amulets addressed to the
child during labor have been tied together in "Come forth."

Sometimes I found that texts needed to be adapted or
transformed to speak more usefully today. The original "silim-
ma" prayer is polytheistic, and is here transformed into our
monotheist idiom (Silim-ma). In some prayers, like "Aneni,"
the original lines, composed for a different purpose, need only
be translated in a new context to become birth prayers. In
"Aneni," I use an old liturgical form and provide new verses
and antiphon. Sometimes the ancient form of a text offends
our modern sensibilities because of androcentricity or xeno-
phobia; with transformation, though, it can cast a brilliant
light on the act of pregnancy ("Shaddai"). Even prayers written
to be recited by women often speak to us across a great con-
ceptual gap, and the translation can be enhanced by a modern
response ("On Reading Ancient Prayers").

The translations, paraphrases, and adaptations in this
book all deal with ancient texts relating to childbirth. But
these texts address only dread and danger. There are other
issues that we wish to address today; to answer these, we have
to look in ancient texts that were not written specifically for
childbirth. This is an unbounded search, involving as much of
our literature as we can master. We read with new eyes, and

individual verses often take on new resonance. Sometimes the texts discuss the issues that come up in pregnancy, such as roundness or blood or pain, in relation to other events and issues. We need to find the language and ideas and recombine them to produce a spiritual understanding that is biblically based and in harmony with the rest of our biblically based religions. This analysis and re-evaluation is a bit like the splicing of genes to create subtly new biological organisms, and we might call it "recombinant theological engineering."

Some of the poems in this volume are meditations sparked by a single verse; others are built around collages of texts centered around a single theme. And some simply find their inspiration in a symbol, story, or concept from our religious heritage.

I have ranged widely in the entire stream of Western religious tradition to find the language to express the sacred dimensions of childbirth. I have used the symbols and traditions that resonate with my own spirituality as a late twentieth-century progressive American Jew with a special fondness for the ancient Sumerians and Akkadians. In this search, I have not respected such cultural boundaries as preBiblical/Biblical; Jewish/Christian; magical/superstitious/religious. I believe that the shared experience of women transcends such cultural and religious boundaries. I include Ancient Mesopotamia as the wellspring of Western cultural tradition, the earliest in which we can trace the written record. Because these ancients wrote on clay, some of the symbols and rituals of such personal affairs as pregnancy and childbirth have survived to come down to us.

For me it also seems natural to cross the boundaries between Christianity and Judaism in my search for religious treasure. I conduct my search in the Western religious tradition because I am steeped in these traditions: I read their languages, know their history, and feel myself a part of the ongoing unfolding of that part of human civilization that stretches from Mesopotamia to America. I do not read Asian, African, and Native-American traditions with the same sense of familiarity. I can appreciate them and learn from them, but I can not give voice to them here as spiritual resources for women in the midst of pregnancy and childbirth. I write out of my sense of my own spirituality and claim all of Western Culture as my spiritual heritage. I realize that many do not draw their own spiritual net as widely as I do. Some Christian women may not find all the Jewish material in the book to have resonance for them, nor will all Jewish women find the Christian material helpful. They may choose to read selectively, and I hope they will not be offended by my own exploration of the full scope of my Western cultural heritage.

Similarly, I often find myself immersed in "magical" or "superstitious" literature. The magic in this book is all religious, focused on praying to God to help. It is "magical" literature in that it is written on amulets, which serve as the visible and tangible component of the prayer. The amulet wearer has an underlying belief that the amulet will accomplish its purpose, just as the worshipper has an underlying hope that God will answer prayer. But with both amulets and prayer, the focus is always God's power to produce the desired effect. Magical texts often reflect the lives and concerns of people, for it is at moments of personal physical and spiritual crisis that people come to practitioners and commission the writing of an amulet. These magic texts, like all religious writing, use symbolic, metaphorical language. God is neither man nor woman, but I sometimes envision God as a human being, a being one is comfortable talking to. I am a faithful monotheist, believing that monotheism best captures the strong sense of unity that I feel in the cosmos. But my experience of the world and of the Sacred is frequently direct and beyond rational; to express this experience, I need mystical and symbolic images. When I set

Sanvai, Sansanvai, and Semongolof to chase away the child-snatcher, they express my sense of dread and danger and my determination to overcome them; when I invoke the aid of Michael and Gabriel, I invoke spiritual power, but I do not expect invisible personalities to be at my side. In the same way, a woman is neither a boat, nor a city, nor the mountains of Jerusalem, nor a prison, nor a universe, nor the Holy Temple, nor an ocean, nor a rocking warchariot, nor Egypt, nor God. But each metaphor increases our ability to understand the implications of pregnancy and to enrich the experience.

This symbolic nature of religious understanding lends itself naturally to poetry, for we tend to read narrative in a far more literal way than we read poems. Moreover, the poems sometimes lend themselves to rituals. We can feel reality with our bodies as well as with our words, we can learn it with our actions even more sharply than from a page. Rituals imprint our prayerful thoughts and wishes on our bodies. Pregnancy should also be enriched by preparatory activities and by beautiful physical objects, such as decorative keys, circle jewelry, birthing robes, and wall plaques that visually enhance our awareness of the Sacred during pregnancy and help us feel the Presence.

Will the sacralization of childbirth make it any easier? Strangely enough, the answer may be yes. Modern holistic medicine continually uncovers more and more connections between the mind and the body. It should not surprise us that hormones caused by stress have immediate bodily impact on the progress of labor. But avoiding pain and speeding labor are not the prime purposes of uncovering the sacred dimensions of pregnancy and childbirth. Childbearing is a holy act. Women who choose to bear have a right to acknowledge the holy implications of their sufferings and their pleasures even when such ideas do not have a measurable physical impact. It is a great blessing to be mindful of the presence of God and the unseen dimensions of life that surround us. The mother's body nourishes and forms the baby. This book is a step toward nourishing and forming the mother.

The months of pregnancy are an ongoing experience of a truly awesome dimension of reality. Inside, beyond our sight, our bodies are doing something that is not quite within our ability to control. Our mind could not isolate, plan, and supervise all the millions of operations that it takes to form and nourish a child. This our body does without conscious direction, through a power that transcends our cognitive mind. To me, this power is the immanent force of God, the presence of divine Presence. We become aware that our very lives depend on this same power, for our bodies perform the manifold operations of circulating the blood, regulating breathing, burning energy and firing synapses in the same "automatic" way. The making of another human being should be an occasion for realizing the sacred holiness of all life. Pregnancy is an intensification of life itself, and all the many experiences of the Holy in human life are sharpened and condensed into the short months in which we engage the future within ourselves.

I have recognized the sacred dimensions of the ordinary experience of a normal pregnancy, and have sought to bring these dimensions to the surface so that others can be mindful of them. It has been my privilege to learn them and teach them, to study and proclaim the Holy with all the art and wisdom I can command.

## IN THE WATERS OF INTERCOURSE
## A BABYLONIAN BIRTH INCANTATION

In the waters of intercourse,
bones were created.
With tissue of muscle,
the birthling was formed.

In the waters of the turbulent and fearful sea,
In the waters of the distant sea,
where the child's limbs are tied,
into the midst of which
the eye of the sun does not shine—
there the god Asarluhi saw him.
He opened the bonds
by which he was bound.
He prepared the road for him,
opened the route.

The way is open for you,
the way is clear.
She will assist you,
She the creator,
She who created us all.

To the locks she will say,
"Be loosened,"
the door sills are apart,
the door is raised.

As a desired child,
bring yourself forth.

# 1. MENSTRUATION

Human life progresses from birth through babyhood, child-hood, adolescence, mature youth, full maturity, old age, and death. This process can be slowed down or speeded up; it can never be stopped or reversed. History and life travel time in a line from the past to the future. But alongside this time is another, nonlinear, cyclical time: the sun rises and sets, the moon waxes and wanes, the seasons come and go. And our bodies also ebb and flow: we sleep and awake, we eat and get hungry, we drink and get thirsty. As these cycles repeat, we are reminded that we are bodies as well as minds, that we live in the natural world and should be mindful of our part in it. Our spiritual lives also have their yearly cycles, as our faith communities relive ritually those moments in our history that are never past, that live eternally and continue to give us life.

Menstruation is a cyclical experience of time, a reminder that the blood of life ebbs and flows throughout the march of history. It is also the sign that women have a particular role to play in this history, that as the generators of humankind they engage in sacred work. Blood is not an ordinary substance: it contains and symbolizes the life force that animates us. Its presence signifies life, and marks its passing away. Blood had a very special use in biblical Israel. It purified Aaron and his sons, the altar, and the Holy of Holies. In other words, the blood of life purified the center in which the collective life of the people received its renewal. This sacral use of blood has a striking parallel to menstruation. A woman's womb is a sacred center, touched with the divine purpose of assuring the continuation of human life and the perpetuating of God's image on this earth. Menstruation is its monthly cleansing.

## BLOOD THE PURE

*My grandmother*
*    and my grandmother's grandmother*
*    and all our grandmothers*
*since eons forever*
*believed my blood unclean.*

*Do I know better?*
*    for my doctors*
*    and my teachers*
*    and my doctors' teachers*
*have explained*
*that the flow is a cleansing,*
*removing from my body*
*matter unneeded*
*which can only decay.*

*And surely I knew,*
*or should have known*
*    that my blood was a cleansing.*
*For it cleansed the altar*
*    at the time of sacrifice,*                    (Lev. 1:5, 11; 3:2, 8, 13.)

*purified the altar at the time of dedication,* (Exod. 29:20f; Lev. 8:15.)
*sprinkled the altar at the time of atonement,* (Lev. 4.)
*and anointed the clothes*
  *of Aaron and his sons*
  *at their consecration.* (Lev. 8:23–24.)


*Blood splattered*
  *on the horns of the altar*
  *purified it.* (Lev. 8:23–24.)
*Blood poured*
  *on the base of the altar consecrated it.* (Lev. 8:15.)
*Blood sprinkled*
  *on the mercy seat implored it.* (Lev. 15:14.)
*Blood,*
*which I have been taught*
*to hide so carefully,*
*purifies the sacred.*
*Purifies me.*


## BLOOD OF THE COVENANT

We often mark our solemn contracts and partnerships with blood. Jewish boys enter the covenant at eight days by the ritual of circumcision. The rare child born without a foreskin, or a convert to Judaism who has already been circumcised for nonreligious reasons, enters the covenant with a ritual that "sheds the blood of the covenant," i.e., draws a single drop of blood from the penis.

When women create, they do not create alone: they create in partnership with men and with God. This partnership is also marked by the shedding of blood.

*When Moses brought the people to Sinai,*
*when he told the people the words of the Lord,*
*then the people agreed to do the Lord's commands.*

*Moses took the blood of oxen.*
*He threw blood on the people, saying*
    "Behold the blood of the Covenant
    Which the Lord has made with you."    (Exod. 24:6–8.)

*Behold the blood of the covenant,*
*for in the sprinkling of blood,*
*you and I are bound together.*

*Come, let us make a pact:*
    *We will sign our names in blood;*
    *we will cut our veins, our fingers,*
    *we will let our blood mingle—*
*Now we are blood brothers,*
*sisters in blood forever.*

*The little Jewish boy,*
*The would-be Jewish man,*
*sprinkles his blood for his covenant with God,*
*sprinkles his blood for the covenanted people.*
    *One drop of genital blood seals the covenant.*
    *One drop of genital blood bonds the male forever.*

*But I, who shed many drops every month,*
    *—What covenant do I affirm?*
    *—What contract do I enter into?*
    *—What bond have I made?*

*Not the covenant of Sinai,*
*not the covenant of Abraham,*
        *—though in these too I may be bound.*

*In my sprinkling of the monthly blood,*
*I am bonded to all women.*
*The covenant of women and God,*
        *ever-eternal, ever-present, everlasting,*
*the covenant sealed in our monthly blood.*

*Our covenant of creation,*
*partners in the handiwork of creation,*
        *for Eve created a child with God.*                    (Gen. 4:11.)
*Our covenant*
*ever renewed,*
*sealed in the monthly blood.*

# 2. Quest

Once, menarche was followed quickly by marriage (when, indeed, it was not preceded by it), and marriage was soon followed by childbirth. In contemporary America, many young teenagers bear children. Nevertheless, as a culture, we prefer a lengthy adolescence. We expect women and men to be competent adults before they marry and hope that they will learn how to live with each other before they have children. Most people marry long after puberty, and then, after being married a few years, are ready to actualize the potential that has been there since puberty. The couple is prepared to conceive; the woman is eager to get pregnant.

It is not always that easy. Infertility has long plagued people, who have tried many folk remedies and prayed for children. For many, pregnancy is an elusive goal. Months and years go by as couples try method after method to conceive. Women who are not trying to become mothers become pregnant, it seems, in an instant. But other women and their partners have to try every method known to technology. Seeking fertility can consume a couple's time, take over their sex life, and dominate their whole relationship. Retaining a sense of sanctity is a struggle as they undergo the mechanization of sex and the invasive procedures of the quest for fertility.

# Prayers and Intercessors

Both Jewish and Christian traditions have produced prayers and customs to promote fertility and induce conception. Women frequently turn to the same intercessory figures whose help they ask during pregnancy and childbirth. In Judaism this is primarily Mother Rachel, the spirit of the beloved biblical matriarch who was long barren and then died bearing her second child. Rachel is buried just outside of Jerusalem on the road to Bethlehem, and her tomb has long been the site of pilgrimage and prayer. Women trying to conceive come and wrap a red string seven times around the tombstone; they wear the string as a fertility charm or as an aid to delivery and will sometimes pray for conception, vowing to bring the child to the tomb when it reaches a certain age. Wearing the string, it is believed, can even help a woman who cannot go to the tomb.

In the Christian tradition, the heavenly mother is, of course, Mary, and women pray to Mary for help in both conception and childbirth. A characteristic prayer is printed in a currently available mother's manual.

> *Mother of Christ, you know, as no other mother can, the high dignity of motherhood. You know how immensely great is the privilege to call into this world a tiny soul destined to praise God forever in heaven.*
> *This is the privilege I now seek, Mary!*

*Confidently I beg you to assist me, for I know that motherhood is so precious in your sight. And confidently, too, I hope for this blessing through your divine Son, since Jesus is the lover of the little children and has said that we should allow them to come to him.*

*It is for this blessing that I beg you to join to my petitions your own holy intercession, that I might be privileged to bring to Jesus a little one such as he so dearly loves, that he may bless it, that he may bless me, also, in my motherhood and that he may then make us both grow in the wonders of his divine life.*
*Mother of Mothers*
*Pray for me.*

The Catholic tradition has also adopted St. Gerard Majella as "the mother's saint" to whom they can turn with prayers for conception and safe pregnancy. St. Gerard was a lay brother who was distinguished by his trust and obedience to God's will. He became known as a miracle worker during his lifetime, and stories of miracles multiplied after his death in 1755. His popularity as the patron of childbirth spread out from Italy, and devotion to him is quite widespread. If you enter a Catholic store in Philadelphia today and ask for an aid to conception, you will be given a Holy Card for St. Gerard which has the following prayer inscribed on its back:

### PRAYER FOR MOTHERHOOD

*O good St. Gerard,*
*powerful intercessor before God and wonderworker of our day,*
*I call upon thee and seek thy aid.*
*Thou who on earth didst always fulfill God's designs,*
*help me to do the Holy Will of God.*
*Beseech the Master of Life from whom all paternity proceedeth,*
*to render me fruitful in offspring,*

*that I may raise up children to God in this life*
*and heirs to the Kingdom of His Glory in the world to come.*
*Amen.*

The use of this Holy Card is quite widespread, and the same prayer has been reported on Holy Cards from Newfoundland. The card, with its prayer, will be used throughout pregnancy.

# The Prayer of Hannah

The Bible records how the barren Hannah prayed for a child:

> *In her wretchedness, she prayed to the Lord, weeping all the while, and she made this vow: "O Lord of Hosts, if you will look upon the suffering of your handmaiden and will remember me and not forget your handmaiden, and if you will grant your handmaiden a human seed, I will dedicate him to the Lord all the days of his life and no razor will ever touch his head" and she kept on praying before the Lord.*
>
> (Sam. 1:10–12)

Why was this prayer heard, this petition granted? Did the vow bring the birth of Samuel? Were the prayers that surrounded this vow particularly effective? In rabbinic literature, Hannah's silent prayer became the prototype and paradigm for all personal prayers. The Rabbis imagined the content of this prayer. In the Babylonian Talmud, Hannah comes to God as a supplicant begs for bread at a banquet:

> *Said Hannah before the Holy Blessed one:*
> *"Master of the Universe, with all the hosts upon hosts*
>     *that you have created in your world,*
>     *is it so hard in your eyes to give me one child?"*

*The matter is like a king of flesh and blood who made a feast for*
    *his servants.*
*One poor man came and stood in the door and said to them,*
    *"Give me a piece of bread,"*
    *and they paid no attention to him.*
*And he went to the king and said,*
    *"M'lord King, with all this feast that you have made,*
    *can you not give me one piece?"*

Hannah in the Talmud reads scripture very closely. In Numbers 5:11–21, a woman whose husband suspects her of adultery has to drink a special potion: "If she is innocent and has not defiled herself, then she is acquitted and she will bear seed." Hannah sees how to use this ritual to her own advantage, threatening God that if she does not get pregnant she will seclude herself innocently so that she will drink the potion and "bear seed."

*Hannah said,*
*"If you do not regard me—*
*then I will seclude myself before Elkanah, my husband.*
*Then as one who secludes herself*
*they will make me drink the waters of the wayward wife*
*and you cannot falsify your Torah. . . ."*

The Talmud also presents Hannah as a natural theologian:

*Hannah said before the Holy Blessed One:*
*"Master of the Universe,*
*there is a host above and a host below . . .*
*If I am from the heavenly host—I should not eat or*
    *drink or give birth or die but live forever . . .*
*just as they live forever.*

*And if I am from the host below—I should eat and drink*
   *and give birth and die."*

She also argues from the design of the female body:

*She said before him,*
*"Master of the Universe, of all that you have created in woman,*
*nothing is without purpose;*
*eyes to see and ears to hear, a nose to smell, a mouth*
   *to speak, hands with which to do work, feet to*
   *walk, breasts to suckle.*
*The breasts that you have placed on my chest—*
*for what purpose are they? not to suckle with them?*

*Give me a child and I will suckle with them."*

# Prayers for Conception

Jewish ritual life provides three opportunities for prayers for conception: at the ritual immersion that traditionally follows menstruation and precedes the resumption of marital sexual relations; before sexual intercourse; and anytime when conception is not forthcoming. An Italian Jewish prayer book for women, handwritten around 1700, contains the following prayer, to be recited after the monthly ritual immersion. Because of the belief that people's thoughts at the time of intercourse determine the nature of the child, the woman prays that she will have the proper thoughts to have a wise and pure child.

*May it be Your will, my God and the God of my fathers,*
*the God of Abraham, the God of Isaac, the God of Jacob,*
*that You should be gracious unto me this night,*
*that I should conceive from my husband,*
*and that the child that is born to me from this immersion*
*will be a wise scholar who fears God*
*and observes Your commandments, rules and laws for themselves.*

*Master of the Universe,*
*receive my prayer and place in my innermost parts*
*a shining pure and holy soul.*
*And let me not defile myself—God forbid—with improper children.*
*And take away from me every strange thought,*
*and save me from evil inclination,*
*so that it cannot tempt me with evil thoughts.*

*And may my husband have good thoughts*
*when he wants to have congress with me,*
*and may he be happy and good-hearted and be gracious with me*
*so that we should have a pure and good-hearted child.*
*And may all my thoughts be such*
*that I should be worthy that my prayers be received before You,*
*for You are the one God,*
*true and faithful,*
*who receives the prayers of Your creatures.*
*Amen*

The Yiddish-language prayer tradition, known as the *tekhines*, also has prayers for this night. In this one, the woman recalls the many times that God has worked miracles through water:

*O Great God!*
*Through water you have made great miracles many times:*

*The righteous Noah was saved from the flood water.*
*Our teacher Moses was drawn forth out of the water.*
*The well of Miriam went with Israel through the desert bringing*
    *water.*
*Show today also your miracle that I should be helped through this*
    *water*
*to have a child,*
*one who will be completely righteous,*
*who will study Torah day and night,*
*who will light my path—after many days—straight to Heaven.*
*May I, through his merit, be worthy*
*to sit with the matriarchs in the women's section of the world-to-*
    *come.*
*Amen.*

For the night of intercourse, Nahmanides, an important medieval Jewish mystical thinker, wrote a prayer for the man to recite that has been preserved in later Jewish prayer books. In this prayer, the man first prays for strength and virility. He then turns to procreation:

*May it be Your will, Rock of all ages,*
    *for the sake of Your great holy Name*
    *as the verse reads, "the Lord remembers us and will*
        *bless us"*
*that You will give me a new seed, a holy seed,*
    *desirable, proper, good, beautiful,*
    *arranged and received and fitting to live*
    *and to endure without guilt or blame,*
*and You will bless me with Your name, and bless my house*
*and I will know that there is peace in my tent*
*and You will let my seed endure*
    *and all the springs from Israel's source. . . .*

*Make my seed whole*
*and let it grow and live and be well formed*
*and may it act rightly and properly and survive. . . .*

*And bless me with the blessings of the skies above and the deep*
*    below*
*and in Your blessings may the house of Your servant be blessed*
*    forever.*

*Amen forever. Selah*

Prayers to remedy childlessness are not limited to these occasions. *The Kitsur Shelah*, an East European compendium of instructions from the early eighteenth century, provides for a ritual to be performed, preferably in Sivan, the month of the giving of the Torah. The husband and wife should fast, arrange the affairs of their house, give money to proper poor people, and recite the following prayer, which concentrates on the fact that God commanded humans to multiply. If God commanded this, then God should make conception possible. Moreover, if God gave the Torah to people to guard, then there must be people:

*You are the Lord Our God.*
*You were our God before You created the world*
*and You are our God from the time You created the world*
*and for eternity You are God.*
*You have created Your world so that Your divinity will be known*
*    in it*
*through the means of Your holy Torah . . .*

*O Lord our God, You wrote two commands in Your Torah:*
*"Be fruitful and multiply"*

*and You wrote in Your Torah*
*"You shall teach this to Your children"*
*and the meaning of both is the same:*
*for You have not created the world as a wilderness,*
*but for inhabiting,*
*and for Your glory you have created, formed and made it,*
*so that we and our offspring*
*and the offspring of all Your people Israel*
*all of us should know Your name and learn Your Torah.*

*And so I come to You, O Lord King of king of kings*
*and I cast my petition before You*
*and my eyes depend on You*
*that You should be gracious to me and hear my plea*
*to bring for me sons and daughters*
*and they too should be fruitful and multiply,*
*they and their children and their children's children*
*till the end of all the generations,*
*For the purpose that we all will be busy with Your holy Torah*
*to study and to teach and to guard and to perform it.  .  .  .*

# Cosmic Union

The attempt to get pregnant is a quest for union, and is like the other occasions when we feel ourselves yearning to join with another, be it God, or another being. Love poetry and song give voice to our desire for each other; the writing of mystics often expresses the yearning of the soul (female) for God and the quest for union with God. The mystics also speak of God's desire for union with us, and, in the language of the mystical Kabbalah, the desire of the holy Being to become truly one by bringing together the two segregated parts of the divine essence, the Holy One Blessed be He and the Presence, the *Shekhinah*, (conceived of as female), and become truly one. The search for conception is another search for such union. Sometimes the act that brings on the fusion of egg and sperm is physical congress between a male and a female; sometimes it is a laboratory procedure in a test tube; sometimes a technical undertaking in a medical setting. In all cases, the conception is a fusion of the sort that provides the energy of the universe.

## YIHUD (UNION)

*There is a math in the cosmos,*
$1 + 1 = 1.$
*The coming together in fusion*
    *of bodies*
    *of souls*
    *of atoms.*
    *of cells.*
*The release of great energy*
    *the intensity of fire*
    *the heat of merging.*

*Even God seeks such fusion,*
*as the Holy Blessed One unites with the Presence.*
*Holy and Holy*
*Hidden and Deep,*
*Primeval Returning, eternal.*

*My soul cries out for You,*
*my Creator,*

*my partner,*
*my God.*
*I yearn to feel my spark*
*join for an instant the mighty flame.*
*I search deep within me, opening myself to Your Presence.*
*Image and form calling the One.*


*In love I join with you,*
*my lover,*
*my partner,*
*my other.*
*Eros opening our bounds,*
*we whirl into a spiral,*
*two axes of a single consciousness.*
*My body opens and embraces,*
*encircles,*
*reaches in yearning,*
*in joy,*
*in love.*


*Inside there is a mighty tumult as fluids roil.*
*My egg is there,*
*its surface sticky, ready to hold on.*
*It reaches to grasp you,*
*you swim toward me,*
*sending out your filaments,*
*to bridge the distance.*
*One little molecule on the egg,*
*one little protein on the sperm—*
*a lock and a key.*


*We dance the dance of life.*
*We intertwine in love.*

*We reach and open:*
*outward searching,*
*inward drawing.*

*May this dance of life journey inward.*
*Deep inside,*
*in tiny form*
*in microscopic cells.*
*May the sperm bridge,*
*the egg envelop.*
*Bonding,*
*fusion,*
*yihud.*
*Let the energy released create a child.*

# With Help

The quest for a child may involve all kinds of diagnostic tests, laparoscopies, surgery, medicines, hyperovulation, GIFT. This search often crowds out passion, spontaneity, and relaxation. Yet couples persevere, determined to create a child. On the way they begin to sense some of the intricate demands that we place on our bodies to actualize our desires. They may have to go through the arduous traumas of technological intervention, often an experience of helplessness and passivity.

It might be helpful to remember that the creation of woman was no less arduous. Genesis describes how God first created all the animals and brought them to Adam but did not find a suitable companion for Adam in that way. So God put

Adam in a deep trance and created Eve out of a totally passive Adam.

### AS AT THE CREATION OF EVE

*When Adam awoke and found the hole in his side,*
*did he feel violated?*
*Did he feel that God should have let him be conscious?*
*Did he want to participate*
*—at least by awareness—*
*in the creation of Eve?*

*Did he feel that he was now less than he had been before?*
>    *missing a side, a rib*
>    *or his dignity?*
*or was the goal of companion*
*and the sight of Eve*
*enough to assuage his longing?*

*Into the hands of others, I commend my body,*
*into the minds of others, I deliver my trust.*
*I remember my love and my desire.*
*May they consider my being,*
*may we all bring life.*

# To Open the Lock

In our search for conception, we seek to open the womb. Then we seek to close the womb to prevent premature pregnancy. Then we seek to open it for conception. Then we seek to close it again to prevent miscarriage. Then we want to open it again for birth, and then to close it again to prevent hemorrhage. So many openings and closings to the door of the womb, so many times we bid our body conform to our calendars. So many times we try to control the body's behavior.

A door opens and closes with a lock and a key. Such a key is in the hand of God. It is God who has the power to open and shut the womb. As the Babylonian Talmud says:

> *Rabbi Yohanan said:*
> *"Three keys were not entrusted to an agent,*
> *and they are, of a birthing woman, of rain, and of*
> *    the resurrection of the dead."*
> *For a birthing woman: "And God listened to her*
> *    and opened her womb"* (Gen. 30:22);
> *of rain: "the Lord will open for you his good*
> *    treasure, the heaven, to give the rain of your*
> *    land in its season"* (Deut. 28:12);
> *of resurrection: "and you will know that I am the*
> *    Lord when I open your graves"* (Ezek. 37:13).
> *In the west they speak also of a key of sustenance,*
> *    "for you open your hand and willingly satisfy*
> *        all living beings"* (Ps. 145:16).

We meet the key of birth in the hand of God in amulets to be worn during pregnancy, in prayers to be recited in later pregnancy and during childbirth, and in the keys of synagogues and churches that Europeans brought to women to hold during labor. Here we invoke it as a symbol for opening the womb for conception. Perhaps we should make the symbol concrete, holding on to or focusing on a key to remind us and help us concentrate on the sanctity of the quest for a child

and on the ultimate goal that transcends the sometimes imper-
sonalizing details of the search.

## THE KEY

*I am the garden locked,*
*a fountain sealed*
*a sealed-up spring.*                                    (Song of Songs 4:12)
*Like the women in the Court of Abimelech,*
*my womb is stopped up.*                                 (Gen. 20:18)
*There is no entry.*

*Once, while Rachel waited*
*God opened Leah's womb.*                                (Gen. 29:31)
*Still, while Rachel waited,*
*ten sons were born to Jacob.*
*Other people have children,*
*other women conceive.*
*Rachel waited*
*and we wait still.*
*We wait and search:*
*Are there mandrakes for us?*

*I know not what closes my womb.*
*Is it the spell of some long-ago wizard?*
*Is it the eye of an envious person?*
*Is it a scar from some once-endured illness?*
*The gift of a poisonous toxin?*

*Three keys are in your hand, God,*
*not entrusted to servants or agents:*
*the key of birthing,*

*the key of rain,*
*and the key of bringing the dead to life.*

*It is time for the key of birthing.*
*Bring it to us*
*to undo the lock.*
*Hear our prayer,*
*open my womb,*
*for life.*

# 3. FORMATION

The first months of pregnancy can be tumultuous. An entirely new being is beginning. The pregnant woman's body has to change to accommodate this new being. She is often exhausted or ill during these months but, at the same time, she may become aware of the great cosmic forces operative in the creation of a child. During the first trimester, a prospective mother often recognizes the enormity of the events happening within her and acknowledges the great demands this new being is now placing on her and will continue to place on her throughout life. At the same time, she must cope with the two faces of abortion: she must decide if she is capable of continuing and willing to continue to create a child; and she must be cognizant of the fact that even if she is willing, something may happen, and the child may be aborted beyond her control. The emotional life of many pregnant women during the first trimester is a kaleidoscope of awareness, ambivalence, assent, and anxiety.

# Beginning III

One day, a woman begins to suspect that she might be pregnant. The herald of this news is likely to be, not an angelic or prophetic messenger, but some of life's more unpleasant sensations: nausea, dizziness, hunger, and exhaustion. The woman asks, "Am I pregnant—or is it something I ate?" "Is it a baby—or is it the flu?" The beginnings of life's miracle or a collapse into illness—the effect on a woman is often the same. Even women who have looked forward to the pregnancy with eager anticipation (and certainly women for whom the pregnancy is a surprise) must question why the creation of life has to be accompanied by such unpleasantness.

This question returns throughout pregnancy, for these nine months, while happy and even blissful for many women, can also be a time of great physical trial. Stomachs ache, feet hurt, headaches and heartburn abound. Numb fingers, swollen ankles, and painful backs are all part of the experience of pregnancy. And then comes labor, an extended moment when pain seems the only present reality and time stops for each contraction.

Something really seems wrong with the morality of the world. Ought not women, who are striving toward continuing our existence, be rewarded with something other than discomfort and pain? Should there not be pleasure in pregnancy as there is in conception? We are often under the illusion that we will be protected while doing good, rewarded for our labors. The nausea, exhaustion, and pain of early pregnancy serve clear notice that matters are not always that simple, that even the most righteous of actions entail hardship and suffering. This is our reality in our not-so-perfect human world.

There is another dimension to the struggles of early pregnancy. The mother's body is performing a phenomenal task. In these early months of pregnancy a fertilized egg changes from a cell to a zygote to an embryo and, finally, to a fully formed miniature fetus. The fertilized egg has the genetic potential to turn into a person, but it is not yet a human being. During the early months of pregnancy, the embryonic stage of the life inside, the cells must be differentiated, the many parts of the body developed, the chemical regulators of body activities composed. The mother not only feeds and protects this life, she actively forms it by the functions of her own body. This is an act of the creation of life, and it is being performed by the woman, in the early months of pregnancy. The woman's body performs an incredible task and must constantly adapt and monitor its own functioning in order to achieve the creation of the fetus.

The woman acts in partnership with God. When the first mother, Eve, looked upon Cain, she said, "I have created a man with God" (Gen. 4:2). God the creator is an active partner in the creation of each child. The Bible recounts how God sees and fashions the child in the womb of the mother. The Talmud elaborates:

> There are three partners in humanity and these are they:
> The Holy Blessed One and the father and the mother.
> The white seed that the man gives: from it comes the bones
>     and the ligaments and the brain cells and the
>     fingernails and the whites of the eyes.
> The red seed that the woman gives: from it come the skin and
>     the flesh and the blood and the black of the eyes.
> From the Holy Blessed One comes the spirit and the breath
>     and the look of the features,
>     wisdom, knowledge, understanding and sight.

The science here is ancient and outmoded, but the passage conveys an appreciation of the divine presence in pregnancy. The pregnant woman harbors the Presence of God in her womb. There is a sense in which we all harbor divinity at all times, for we all harbor a spark of divine essence. But at the time of pregnancy, an additional Presence comes to her womb, the sacred power that creates life.

### SACRED PRESENCE

It begins.
Deep within.
Stormy encounters,
fusions,
explosions,
divisions,
embedding.

A titanic effort has begun.
Great powers have been loosed.
A mighty force gathers together,
Divinity works within me.

My body mobilizes:
hormones adjust,
fluids rebalance,
blood flow adapts,
new cells are created.

I am tired.
Nauseated,
puffy and swollen.
A soldier exhausted in the heat of battle,
A doctor wearied by hours on duty,
A laborer on an unending shift,

*A parent on perpetual call:*
*This is hard work.*

*Where are the songs, the harps,*
      *the angels floating on clouds?*
*Where is the sweetness and light?*
*Should not a holy task be pleasant,*
*gentle in the grace of God?*

*Instead, the power of God is upon me;*
*My being joins in the fray,*
*I ache with the effort of the Presence—*
*My song of rejoicing is purchased by pain.*
*God is a difficult partner.*

# Creation

In the body of the woman, a life is taking shape. Cells are forming that will be multiplied into millions of cells, all ultimately to function as a single organism, guided by a single consciousness. Our ancient myths celebrate the process by which our solid and differentiated universe emerged from the primeval fluid mass. The Babylonian Enuma Elish myth relates the merging of Apsu, the sweet-water ocean below the land, and Tiamat, the saltwater ocean. The commingling of their waters led to the emersion of the first creatures, Lahmu and Lahamu. The story of creation in Genesis also refers to the primordial water, which it calls *tohu vevohu*, usually translated as "void and without form." The creation of the cosmos is powered by fusion and fission, and it bears many similarities to the creation of a person. Every person is a whole cosmos, and the life-forming process in the individual human being is the life-forming process of our universe itself. The fertilized egg divides into two, then four, then eight and then sixteen increasingly smaller cells (blastomeres). Then this sixteen-cell conceptus travels to the womb and begins to grow.

*In the depths of the maternal sea,*
*fluids solidify,*
*milk congeals, mud comes from waters.*
*In the heart of the maternal sea,*
*solid emerges from soup:*
*A baby is forming.*
*Flesh of my flesh,*
*bone of my bones,*
*seed of my soul*
*and another.*

*The waters of the void are doubled in one*
*apsu-tiamat,*
*tohu-vavohu,*
*egg and sperm.*

*Chemical processes,*
*fusion reactions,*
*energy releases.*

*One is the beginning;*
*One is the start.*

*Into the oneness of the void comes a two:*
*light and dark,*
*night and day,*
*lahmu-lahamu,*

*heaven and earth.*
*First divisions,*
*polarities,*
*distinctions.*
*The one formed by two becomes once again two,*
*two to be four,*
*four to be eight,*
*eight and eight to 16—*
*the journey begins.*

*In the waters of the mother*
*comes the voyage.*
*Down canals to the ocean*
*deep in the maternal sea.*
*Home to the sea*
*in me.*

## Woman Weaving

In American folklore, a woman often announces her pregnancy to her husband by sitting and conspicuously knitting booties. This image of the pregnant woman knitting is both unrealistic and anachronistic. Nevertheless, it survives in popular culture on television and in cartoons, perhaps because knitting (or weaving or spinning) is a profound metaphor for the endeavor of pregnancy.

Since ancient times, women have been associated with the creation of cloth by spinning, weaving, and knitting. These are activities of the home and can usually be done with children nearby. They are, moreover, transformations of a natural product (wool) into a useful aspect of culture, and such trans-formations of nature into culture are classic jobs of women. Ancient images of women frequently show them holding the distaff and spindle, and both "distaff" (a portable spinning de-vice) and "spinster" became in our language expressions for the female. In Babylon, the gender-destiny of each child was marked by placing into the hand of the newborn girl a tiny spindle and the newborn boy a tiny arrow. Famous tales of women-as-weavers and spinners have come down to us, from Penelope the wife of Odysseus who spent her days weaving and her nights taking apart the work until Odysseus arrived home, to Arachne, the princess whose weaving was so perfect that Athena, jealous, turned her into a spider. In Sumer, Uttu was the weaving goddess, she who was given to humankind to teach them how to make clothes.

There is a profound connection between pregnancy and weaving or knitting—and it goes far beyond their status as "women's work." As far as our eyes can see, a child begins in the liquids of sex. The semen of man, the secretions of women, all are sticky and wet. Then, nine months later, the child comes out as a solid reality. How has a drop of liquid come out so real, so solid? Job suggests it congeals, like cheese (Job 10:8). But a child is much more complex than a hunk of cheese, and Job continues, "You wove me of bones and sinews." This image is also used by the Psalmist, who declares, "You wove me in the recesses of the earth" (Ps. 139:45). They are using a powerful and natural metaphor for child formation: the often intricate and beautifully patterned cloth that is spun, woven, knitted, and embroidered by women at their work.

## SPIDER WOMAN

*An ancient amulet starts:*
*"Once Smamit gave birth to sons,*
*and evil Sideros killed them all"*

*Because of her, the evil one will not kill*
*where the names of her guardians are found.*

*But Smamit is a spider—*
*what have I with spiders?*
*Arachne the spider;*
*Smamit the spider;*
*Tsitsinako,*
*Indian Thought-Woman,*
*also a spider:*
*a spider who thought and wove the world to be.*

*Weaving is the woman*
*—spinning bodies,*
*spinning worlds.*

*Woman weaves the threads,*
*spins the cloth,*
*knits the bodies together*
*in the depths of her being.*
*"Into the hands of a girl-child*
*place the distaff and the spindle."*

*From gossamer comes solidity;*
*from strands, a cloth,*
*from DNA, a human.*

# A Fantasy of Creation

This Jewish midrash, Yetzirat haValed, which probably dates from the eighth century, is a fantasy about the beginning of pregnancy.

*At the hour that a man comes to bed with his wife, the Holy Blessed One says to the angel in charge of pregnancy, "Mr. X is emitting human seed, and you, go and guard that drop, collect it in a cup and thresh it into 365 parts."*

*He brings it before the Holy Blessed One, who decrees whether it will be mighty or weak, long or short, male or female, foolish or wise, rich or poor, but not whether it will be righteous or wicked, as it is written, "Everything is in the hand of heaven except the fear of heaven."*

*Immediately, the Holy Blessed One says to the angel in charge of the spirits, "bring me soul X." It comes before the Holy Blessed One, who says, "Go into that drop."*

*The soul opens its mouth and says, "Master of the Universe, the world that I have been in since I was created is fine for me. If you please, do not make me enter into this stinking drop, for I am pure and holy." The Holy Blessed One says, "the world that I am making you enter is better than the world where you have been, and when I created you, I created you especially for this drop" and places it in the drop against its will.*

*The angel returns the spirit into the belly of its mother and invites two angels to guard it so that it doesn't fall out. They leave a lamp lit over its head . . . and it sees from the beginning of the world until its end.*

*In the morning the angel takes it to paradise and shows it the righteous sitting in glory, and says, "The one that you see in such glory and exaltation was created like you in the belly of its mother,* as was that one and that one, and they observed the laws and rules of the Holy Blessed One. If you do as they did, then, after you die, you will merit this glory and exaltation which you see; if not, then your end is to go to the place which I will show you."

In the evening he takes it to hell and shows it the evil ones whom the angels of suffering are beating and hitting with rods of fire. They are yelling, "Oy Vavoy," but nobody has compassion on them. The angel says to it, "Know that these were created from a stinking drop in their mother's belly and went out to the world. They didn't observe the laws of the Holy Blessed One and so they came to this shameful end. And now, my child, know that your end is to die. Do not be an evil one, but be righteous and live in the next world."

He journeys with it from morning till evening and shows it every place that its foot will walk and where it will live and where it will be buried and afterwards shows it the world of the good and the bad.

In the evening he returns it to the belly of its mother and the Holy Blessed One makes a double door and bolt and says "until here you come and no more."


The fetus stays in the belly of its mother nine months. The first three months it lives in the lower chamber, in the middle three months in the middle chamber and in the last three months in the upper chamber, and it eats whatever its mother eats and drinks from what its mother drinks and doesn't excrete so that its mother won't die.

And when it is its time to go out, the same angel comes and says to it, "The time has come for you to go out to the world," and it says, "I already told the One Who Spoke and the World Came to Be that I felt fine in the world that I was living in. He said, 'The world that I am bringing you into is beautiful and, moreover, against your will you are created in the belly of your mother and against your will you are born and go out into the world.'" Immediately it cries, and why does it cry? For the world which it was in. And when it comes out the angel hits it under its nose and puts out the light over its head and brings it out against its will and it immediately forgets everything.

# The Ground of Being

The pregnant woman can also strike us as a great force of nature: like the very earth itself she is growing new life. Ancient literature speaks of "ploughing" and "tilling" women, with men, of course, the tillers. The Koran calls upon men to act in this way: "your women are your tillage, so come to your tillage as you wish" (2:223). The Talmud indicates the parameters of this metaphor:

> *Resh Lakish said in the name of Bar Kappara:*
> *Scripture says "stopped" up about a woman,*　　　　(Gen. 20:18)
> 　　*and "stopped up" about the sky:*　　　　　　　　(Deut. 11:17)
> *Scripture says "birth" about woman,*　　　　　　　(Gen. 30:23)
> 　　*and "birth" about the earth.*　　　　　　　　　(Isaiah 55:10)
> *Scripture says "took note of" about woman*　　　　(Gen. 21:23)
> *and "took note of" about the earth.*　　　　　　　(Ps. 65:10)

This metaphor is sunk deep in our consciousness, and our modern languages still speak of the "seed" in the ground and in the belly of the woman, still talk of "barrenness" and of "fertility."

Our myths sometimes turn the metaphor around and tell tales of how the first humans grew in the ground like grass. Greek mythology preserves the story of Jason sowing dragon's teeth and the men who grew there. In Sumerian myth, "The Creation of the Pickaxe" tells the tale:

> *Once the earth gave birth to us all,*
> *as the god Enlil opened her with a pickaxe,*
> 　　*placed the seed in the mud,*
> *and the nation sprouted up through the ground.*

The earthy, natural quality of pregnancy sometimes causes people to think of the woman as passive and receptive, the ground of being, who have even been forced to bear children against their will.

But, as Jewish tradition has recognized, women are not the ground. They are human beings, moral agents with the ability, the right, and the obligation to determine their destiny. They must choose their actions and stand responsible for their choices. Pregnancy may be a holy task, but only free human beings can perform a holy task. **One cannot be forced to devote oneself to a service, no matter how sacred.**

To use the metaphor of earth mother is not to imagine that women's part in creation is automatic and passive. Quite the contrary: this comparison may help us to realize that the earth also is a mother, and that the earth also cannot be forced indefinitely. Many complex elements in the earth have to co-ordinate in order to sustain life, just as many complex elements in woman must coordinate to create life.

It might be nice to dramatize the metaphor. We should honor both the mother and the earth as the ground of being. One could plant a sapling during the first trimester in order to symbolize this likeness. And we should pause to acknowledge both the similarity and the difference, for woman is mother—earth only when she chooses to be the ground of being.

> *The farmer plows the field,*
>     *makes furrows in the empty ground,*
>     *forms holes in the earth,*
>     *places seed into the waiting holes.*
> *The farmer tends and nurtures the earth,*
>     *waters it, husbands it,*
>     *prays it be not barren.*
> *The fertile earth bears the harvest.*

*Man plows his woman,*
*deposits his seed.*

*Like earth, woman can be raped.*
*Like earth, woman may be nurtured.*
*Like earth, woman brings forth her harvest of new life.*

*Fertile earth, fertile woman;*
*barren earth, barren woman;*
*mother earth, mother woman.*

*Woman-earth, who brings forth children.*
*Earth-woman, who tends the life inside,*
*cares and tends lives forever.*

*Earth gives us life,*
*woman gives us life.*
*Earth gives us food,*
*woman gives us food;*
     *food from her body,*
     *food from the earth.*

*Women too have seed,*
     *are barren,*
     *are fertile*
     *and bear.*

*"Who will plow my vulva,"*
     *calls the ancient goddess/woman*
*The thrust and lift of the plough in the earth*
*echoes the thrust and lift of a man in a woman.*

*Yet . . . women are not the ground;*
*we cannot be forced to bear.*

*Today I take my choice.*
*Today I state my will:*
*I will be earth to this baby,*
*I will grow this child.*

## Assent

Pregnancy always involves choice, no matter how much cultures seek to deny women the choice. And the choice is not always easy. Even when a woman wants a baby, there may come a time during the pregnancy when she begins to feel that her body has been invaded by another being, colonized by a separate force. Her life is no longer entirely in her control, and she must be ever-mindful of the fact that her most personal decisions—when to sleep, what to eat, what to do— must be made with constant consideration for the welfare of a different, not-quite-separate being.

This feeling of being under another's control is even more acute when the pregnancy is unwanted, when it is a surprise addition to a life full of other commitments, and even more so when the sex itself was forced. Our news, our novels, and our mythology are full of constant reminders that women can become pregnant without intention and can be raped against their will. From Greek women impregnated by swans and showers of gold to the violent assaults of today, the knowledge that this can happen is engraved upon a girl's consciousness even before she is able to read. Even when the pregnancy is fervently desired, the lack of personal autonomy that care for the unborn entails can be a great shock to the pregnant woman, who begins to understand that her life is no longer solely her own, that her decisions must consider the well-being of another.

There is even more to the feeling of being colonized, for this feeling comes with the realization that pregnancy is only the beginning of such surrender to the needs of another. Parenting is a continual act of consideration for the child, and parents routinely perform such acts of self-denial and altruism that, were they performed for any but their own children, would easily qualify them as the sainted righteous of the world. Adjusting our sleep to the demands of the newborn, modifying our activities to conform to the abilities of the toddler, adjusting our schedule to pay attention to children's needs and desires, stretching the budget (and forgoing luxuries) to afford the costs of children's education: in all these, and in many more ways, parents sacrifice or postpone their own desires in order to care for their young.

There is often joy in such giving; but there is also occasional resentment. And those who expect to be paid back by children's gratitude or generosity are often disappointed. We expect ourselves to center our attention on our children—we cannot expect them to center their attention on us. At two, at seven, at eleven, at eighteen, children grow increasingly interested in their own world, less eager to participate in ours. If we are wise, we welcome each succeeding act of self-definition and independence. Our goal is to produce human beings who are capable of caring for themselves and others; we need to give them the ability to see themselves as separate persons—which means that they must detach from us, and we must help them do so. And this is frequently the gift to our children that is the hardest for us to give.

We know all this. Most of us have lived through separation from our own parents. Our culture is full of symbols of the ambiguous, sometimes distant and sometimes stormy relationships between mothers and their children. And yet, we continue to choose to have children and raise them. This very choice, sometimes made before pregnancy, often made during pregnancy, is a great act of heroism and self-sacrifice. Rarely has it been looked upon in this way. Far more often, mother-hood has been treated as the destiny of women, and culture has kept very quiet about women's acceptance of this destiny. The possibility of choice has either been ignored or denied. In the past, when it was technically difficult to abort children (though easy to murder them at birth), women have been treated as though they had no choice. Now, when re-productive technology has made the possibility of terminating a pregnancy technically very easy, society threatens to deny women their choice by legal means. Perhaps this very urge to present pregnancy as a nonchoice imposition represents a subconscious acknowledgement of the enormous sacrifice of self that a woman makes to become a mother and a fear that women will not agree to do so if they have alternatives.

Culture has recorded one woman's choice of pregnancy. The gospel of Luke presents Mary as a simple girl who an-swered "Let it be done" when her pregnancy was announced to her (Luke 1:38). Did she assent *before* she became pregnant or after? The Greek is ambiguous. Would she have remained or become unpregnant if she had said no? The text doesn't say. In the end, what is important is her choice: Let it be done. Often this is explained as an example of the virtue of submission or obedience. But obedience is not a virtue unless there exists the genuine possibility of *not* obeying. The Mary of the Gospels is, above all, a paradigm of the choice of all women. At the same time, Mary is also a model of how thankless motherhood can seem to be, for when Jesus was told that Mary and his brothers were outside trying to see him, he told his assembled listeners that they, rather than Mary, were his true family (Luke 8:19–21).

Later Christian theology has heaped rewards and benefits

on Mary, assigning her an immaculate conception, an assumption to heaven, and a coronation as queen of heaven. The Gospels, however, do not deal with these issues. They present a woman whose glory consists in her choice to accept maternity and whose reward was the fact of that maternity itself, the existence of the son, rather than any homage he might pay her.

## THE VESSEL

*When Mary heard the voice in her ear*
    *and knew that she was pregnant,*
*did she feel abused?*
            *violated?*
            *exploited for her womb?*
*with an alien being growing in her midst?*

*Did she hate the new role that had come upon her,*
*wanting to remain young*
            *unencumbered*
            *at play?*
*Instead of standing slow, and heavy,*
*waiting for the birth.*

*The young girls laugh and play—*
    *what do the mothers do?*
*After the labor of giving birth*
*more work awaits.*
*motherhood comes after childbirth.*

*Every child will disavow its mother—*
    *"Don't kiss me in public"*

*"You're embarrassing me"*
*"I'd rather be with my friends."*

*Knowing all this, as every mother knows,*
*I say, "let it be done."*
*In love, all is possible.*

# Months of Anxiety

The early months of pregnancy, the time when the fetus is being formed, is a time fraught with danger for the fetus. Foods and chemicals that the mother ingests can have a dramatic impact on the ability of the fetus to develop normally. Women are advised to watch what they eat, to avoid alcohol, drugs, and medicines, to keep away from caffeine and nicotine. Moreover, all these precautions may not prevent an early miscarriage, which can be caused by some defect in the fetus itself. This lack of control over the destiny of the fetus does not lead to an absence of worry. On the contrary, the anxiety is there, magnified by our sense of not being in control. Pregnant women are acutely aware that they have not yet given birth to a live child and wrestle with anxiety over the possibility that they may miscarry.

This anxiety will not go away by trying to ignore it. It is a rational fear, for women *do* miscarry. At the same time, it is beyond rational remedy. People tend to respond to the anxiety of pregnant women with such admonishments as "Don't worry—nothing is going to happen," or "Be calm—there is nothing you can do anyway." But such statements deny the reality of the anxiety and invalidate the emotions of the anxious mother (she hopes) -to-be. Anxiety needs to be expressed, alleviated, and worked through. The woman needs to concentrate on her resolve and desire for the baby. The anxiety is both rational and beyond rational; it demands expression by both direct and symbolic words and deeds.

## THE MATRIARCH PRAYER

This Jewish prayer is found in the early modern Hebrew prayerbooks for Italian Jewish women, with the notation that it should be recited from the fortieth day of pregnancy on. The prayer pays special attention to the help that God gave Israel's matriarchs in their desire for children.

*Master of the entire world,*
*Lord of Hosts:*
*the eyes of all turn to you,*
*for in times of trouble our salvation is with you.*

*Even though I am not worthy to come before you in*
        *prayer,*
*I have strengthened myself like steel*
*and come to cast my plea before you:*
*Just as you took note of Sarah*        (Gen. 21:1)
*and you listened to entreaties for Rebecca*     (Gen. 25:21)
*and you looked upon Leah's suffering*       (Gen. 29:31)
*and you remembered our holy mother Rachel*   (Gen. 30:22)
*and you have listened to the prayers of righteous*
        *women forever,*

*so in your manifold mercy look upon my distress*
*and remember me,*
*and harken to the sound of my supplication,*
*and send the redeeming angel to support me*

*and help me during this pregnancy of mine.*
*And for the sake of your mercy,*
*save me and rescue me*
*from all evil.*


There is an official Catholic "Blessing of an Expectant Mother," not well known even in Catholic circles, that addresses the anxiety of women in earlier pregnancy and their hope in Divine protection:


*Lord God, Creator of all,*
*strong and mighty, just and merciful.*
*You alone are all good and kind.*


*You delivered Israel from all evil,*
    *making our fathers pleasing in your sight,*
*and you sanctified them by the hand of your Holy Spirit.*


*You prepared the body and soul of the glorious Virgin Mary*
    *by the cooperation of the Holy Spirit*
*in order that she might be a worthy dwelling for your son. . . .*


*So now receive the sacrifice of a contrite heart*
    *and the fervent desire of this devoted mother,*
*who humbly asks you for the preservation of her child*
    *which you have helped her to conceive.*
*Guard her and defend her from all deceit*
    *and hurt of our bitter Enemy.*
*So that, by the birth-giving hand of your mercy,*
*her child may come happily to the light of regeneration*
*and deserve to be joined to you in all things*
*and merit to gain eternal life . . . Amen.*

*Let us pray:*
*Come, we beg you, Lord, to this dwelling*
*and drive all danger far from it*
*and from this your devoted servant.*

*Let your holy angels dwell here,*
*and let them keep her and her child in peace,*
*and let your blessing be always with her.*
*Save them, almighty God,*
*and grant to them your perpetual light*
*Through Christ our Lord. Amen*

# Counting the Days

Teach us to count our days rightly, that
we may obtain a wise heart—Ps. 90:12

*As I rise, I remember the countings.*
*7 are the days of creation,*
*days of division from chaos to life.*
*7 are the days from the moment of conception*
*to the day you implanted in me,*
*a little new part,*
*burying itself in my womb.*

*I remember other countings.*
*29 are the days of the month of the moon*
*as the moon makes its journeys around our world.*
*So are the days of most menstrual cycles.*
*This time, I do not flow.*
*In my womb, at this time, a streak appears in you—*
*up and down,*

right and left,
your world now has direction.


40 are the days of Lent
40 the days of Elijah on Sinai
40 the days of Jesus in the desert
40 the years of Israel's wanderings.


On the fortieth day I add to my prayers,
"As you have always protected women, protect me."


There are forty days as the nervous system forms.
From the 18th day
to the time when the organs are in place.
These are days of danger and challenge,
the early days of developing life.
These are the days of test and question:
Will you make it?
Will you come through this time intact, in me?


As Israel came through the desert wanderings,
and Elijah came through at Sinai;
as Jesus endured in the desert,
so may you survive this time of ordeal.


Today we count the days till safety,
together we will count the weeks till birth,
together we mark the months till delivery
counting the Omer,
marking the harvest,
marking off the days
till your beginning of time.

# The Circle

During these early months, a round circle begins to appear on the woman's belly. She may greet it with deep pleasure or dread, but there it is, a sign of the developments happening within and a harbinger of the growth to come. It is a biological fact of life—or is it? The round circle on the abdomen of a woman in early pregnancy is not required by the minuscule size of the embryo at this point, nor by the still-small size of the woman. Just as the abdomen in later pregnancy is much larger than the baby that will emerge, so too the early circle is greater than that within it. This roundness is a biological fact of life, but it is not absolutely required by biological reasons and serves as a key indicator of many of the symbolic dimensions of the experience.

In early pregnancy the round circle is a little circle, almost flat, almost like a circle drawn in the sand. These set off a ritual area—the temenos—which is guarded from the outside, preserves that which is in, and serves as the barrier between the world and the sacred. Out of the circle stays all danger, and inside comes the power.

A *little* circle figures in several stories from Jewish midrash. Two are about Moses. In one, Moses stands in a little circle to intercede for Miriam: "I shall not stir from here until Miriam my sister is healed." In the other, Moses stands in a circle to demand not to die. In both of these stories, the circle drawing defines an area in which Moses confines himself and swears to remain confined until God gives in to his demands. The circle defines the area of self-confinement. A similar story is told (in a Talmudic tractate) of the prophet Habakkuk, who drew a circle and proclaimed that he would not stir from there until God told him how long God would tolerate the wicked in this world.

The most famous circle in Jewish legendry was drawn by Honi the circle drawer:

> *The people sent a message to Honi the circle drawer, Pray that rain may fall. He prayed and no rain fell. He then drew a circle and stood within it in the same way that the prophet Habakkuk had done . . . He exclaimed . . . "I pray that I will not move from here until you have mercy on your children."*

Honi stayed in the circle he had drawn, through drizzle and deluge, not moving until God gave him exactly what he asked for.

Biblical poetry records the earliest confining circle. Before God could create our universe, the unruly sea had to be subdued. God did so by drawing a circle and confining the sea within it.

All these circles of confinement suggest that the circle on the mother's abdomen is also there as a visible, enclosed area in which the developing life should stay.

### TEMENOS

*Into the circle I invite You,*
*power of creation,*
*power of form.*
*Into the circle I invoke You,*
*power of life.*

> *As You come into the circle of the sea,*
> *drawn in the sand,*

*power over chaos, power of life,*
*power of distinction, power to do—*
into my circle I invite You.


Moses drew a little circle around him:
"I will not move from here.
In the circle that now surrounds me I stand unmovable—
In this circle, I stay."


Habakkuk drew a circle and stood inside it,
"I shall not stir from here.
Tell me what I want to know—
In this circle, I stay."


Honi the circle drawer also drew a circle:
"I will not move from here.
Listen to me and do my bidding—
In this circle, I stay."


Once a general drew a circle around a king:
"Do not leave," he said.
"Until you are ready to decide,
in this circle, stay!"


God too drew a circle:
on the waters, a place for sea.
To the waves, God said, "Do not leave here:
In this circle, stay!"


And now we draw a circle on my body,
a little circle to surround you.
And now I say—
and may God also say—

*"Till the time has come when you are ready,*
*in this circle, stay!"*

# Holding the Key

The cervix, the door of the womb, must remain closed until it opens to let out a fully formed baby. If this door of the woman opens too soon, the baby is aborted. To prevent this, we pray that the door remain closed, and we look for a key that can close it. Such a key is the key of life in God's hand. The key that opened the womb for conception must now lock the door that it opened.

A key might be a meaningful item of jewelry to give a pregnant woman. The key would symbolize God's key of birthing, and putting it on a chain around her neck or holding it in her hand would be a way for a pregnant woman to focus her attention on her desire for the fetus's safety. Wearing images of the key to the womb has a long history. Pregnant women in Hellenistic Egypt wore rings that showed a womb stylized as an upside-down pot, with a toothed image next to the neck, which was the key. Thousands of years later, an early-modern Hebrew brooch, which was originally a pendant, continues this tradition. One side has a blue stone and the other contains a prayer:

*"O Gracious and merciful God, be gracious and merciful to this woman that she not abort and that the birthling come out at its appropriate time and be healthy (bry)."*

At the bottom is a picture of the key and the word *PTH* ("open"). The wearing of a key amulet does not *work* in the magical sense of really protecting the fetus from abortion. But it is a visible reminder, a tangible prayer to express one's hopes and fears. It is a multicultural symbol, like this poem, where the key symbol is joined by the boat metaphor from Sumer and Babylon and the ark and Jerusalem analogies from the Hebrew bible.

## UNDER LOCK AND KEY

*I place a key on my table,*
*wear a key around my neck,*
*hold a key in my hand,*
*draw a key on my ring.*
> *With the key that opened,*
> *shut fast the lock.*

*My body is like a boat,*
> *its cargo held safe in its midst.*
*My body is like a city,*
> *gates shut for the night,*
> *whose children sleep within.*

*Once, God shut Noah into the ark,*          (Gen. 7:16)
*and kept him from destruction.*
*Now, may I too be locked like a boat—*
> *may my precious cargo be sealed in my hold,*
> *may my portal hold fast till the good hour.*

*Jerusalem praises God,*
*Zion thanks the Lord,*
*For God strengthens the gate of her city,*
*and blesses her children within.*          (Ps. 147:13–14)

*May I be like Zion,*
>  *holy place, site of God's presence,*
>  *mother whose children are blessed.*

*May the key in my hand,*
*and the key in Your hand:*
*fasten the lock till birth.*

# 4. AFFIRMATION

## A Body Grows: Shaddai

By the fourth month, the body of the child has been formed, and our own bodies are undergoing enormous changes. This is an important time to think about the human body. As women, we are often preoccupied with our bodies. Culturally taught to value slimness and grace, we worry that our breasts are too small, or too large; that our waists are too thick or our hips too big or our backsides too flat or too prominent. We may starve or stuff ourselves, or do both in a frustrating and damaging cycle of alternation. We exercise beyond the needs of health, we have our tummies tucked, our breasts augmented, our thighs suctioned, and any other number of "improvements" attempted. Even men are now succumbing to this obsession, worrying not only about their abdomens but also about the size of their pectoral muscles.

But all this is a matter of our figures, our outward appearance. We very rarely think about our *bodies*, the magnificently intricate systems with which we experience life. When the systems malfunction and we experience illness or pain, then we may pay attention, but we are thinking about what is wrong and how to correct it. We very rarely think about all that is right with our bodies.

A very different sense is expressed by Psalm 139:14

*I praise You,*
*for I am awesomely, wondrously made;*
*Your work is wonderful,*
*I know it very well.*

No matter what we look like, no matter if we are young or old, fat or slim, tall or short, fit or flabby, healthy or ill, our bodes are awesomely, wondrously made: they breathe, they digest, they enable us to live life. If, at the same time, they make it possible for us to hear, to see, to talk, to move, or to touch, what a great gift we have. If we can do more than one of these, we should give praise daily for the wonderful work of our creation. And if we can do all of them, we have been greatly blessed.

The human being is not some abstract spirit surrounded by flesh. We don't "have" bodies the way we have clothes: we *are* our bodies. As our life is sacred, so are our bodies; as our spirits manifest the presence of divinity—so do our limbs. The first chapter of the Bible tells us this when God says to the other sacred beings: "Let us create humanity in our image, in our likeness, *betsalmenu kidmutenu.*" Alone, the phrase "in our image" could be ambiguous: *tselem* in ancient Assyrian texts refers to the role of the king as the counterpart of God on earth. The addition of "in our likeness" makes the meaning very clear: humanity looks like God and the other sacred beings. Not only our spirits, but our bodies also are in the likeness of God—and not only perfect bodies, but all human bodies. Male and female, variously colored, aged, sized, and abled, humans are in the likeness of God.

We have learned to be embarrassed by this *"anthropomorphism,"* this imagining that God looks like human beings, and to consider it a primitive way of thinking! After all, if horses would imagine God, the horse-God would have four legs, hoofs, and a mane and tail. Of course the God of human beings has hands and arms, face and back, mouth and nose, ears and eyes! What else would He/She have? How else could we talk about God's actions? These features of God are metaphors by which we can understand our experience of the actions of God. In reality, God is not a Giant in the Sky, or an Old Man with a Beard, or a Young Warrior with Outstretched Arm. Ultimately, we interpret away all scriptural references to the body of God, or limit them to our periods of dream thinking and mystical imaging.

Our own bodies, however, are not metaphors: they are real and ever present in our lives. This raises a theological issue: since we understand that the body of God is symbolic, how can we retain a sense that our bodies are divine and sacred? This dilemma has plagued our religion and philosophy, with the result that we have hated, ignored, and seriously undervalued our bodies. We have treated them as incidental to our essence at the same time that we have seen them as essential to our appearance. It is no wonder that many of us wind up abusing our bodies with chemicals, vomiting, and starvation.

Pregnancy brings the issue of the body into high relief. For many women, it is a time of anguished awareness that the bodies that we have tried so hard to keep concave are becoming convex. It is also a time of physical discomfort: the swollen aching from our ankles to our breasts reminds us of the presence of our body and of its limitations. We are tired, we are hot. We may be off-balance, our back may complain of the load. We stumble easily, walk gingerly, and rise with great difficulty. And at the same time we must be careful what we put into our bodies: the food we eat, the liquids we drink, the medicines we take, the chemicals we come in contact with: all these can affect the development of the unborn child, can damage the new being we are creating. We must find a way to feel comfortable with our bodies in all their new restrictions and limitations; we must discover the path to feeling the wonder of our bodies for the job they are doing in sustaining our lives and in creating others. We must learn to experience our bodies as sacred in all their activities and stages.

This is not only a task for pregnant women. All humans need to confront the reality and the beauty and the divinity of their bodies. But what images can we use, what language can we think with when we no longer understand "in the likeness of God" as a statement of literal fact? One answer may come from an obscure Jewish midrash probably written sometime during the eighth to tenth centuries. In the *Midrash Tanhuma* we read:

> *All of Israel who are circumcised enter Paradise, for the Holy Blessed One placed his name on Israel so that they should enter Paradise. And what is the name and the seal that he placed upon them: "Shaddai." He placed the letter* shin *in the nose, the letter* daled *in the hand, and the* yod *at the circumcision.*

There is much in this early medieval midrash that is offensive to the modern mind. It is totally ethnocentric, not admitting the uncircumcised into Paradise, and it is completely androcentric: What about women? But beyond all that, buried beneath the sexism and the chauvinism, lies a wonderful idea, that the human body carries one of the great names of God, Shaddai. The first Hebrew letter, *shin*, has the shape of the human nose; the second Hebrew letter, the *daled*, of the humanoid hand, a hand that we share with other primates, who should perhaps be treated as special kin to humans. The third Hebrew letter, *yod*, the smallest letter of the Hebrew alphabet, is also the first letter of the divine name YHWH and often stands by itself for an abbreviation of the divine name. It is not circumcision that looks like a *yod*, but the genitalia themselves, both penis and clitoris. The sensitivity of these two genital *yods*, the penis and clitoris, enable us to feel the pleasure of sexuality and to desire each other at any time. This boundless sexuality distinguishes us from the estrus-related activity of other animals. When we realize the significance of the *yod*, the sexism and chauvinism of the medieval midrash fall away and we have a way of seeing the human body bearing the name of God in precisely those features that make it most human. This, in turn, gives new meaning to the phrase in Psalm 118:26: "Blessed be the one who comes in the name of the Lord." This embodied name has been created by the twelfth week of gestation.

### SHADDAI

*It is the twelfth week of gestation,*
*fourteen weeks in the counting.*
*A body grows and becomes.*
*There, on its form, is stamped its destiny:*
*To be a person,*
*image of God,*
*partner in creation,*
*lover of the world.*

*The body in which it will know life*
*is taking shape.*
*On its face, there is a nose.*
*The human nose, beacon of the face.*
*The nose that breathes the air of the world,*
*smells the creation,*
*tastes the pleasures of life.*
*The nose of a human being stretches forward from the face.*
*Not a beak,*

not a snout,
center bone and two nostrils.
the letter shin **ש**   sha.

From the body stretch forth the arms and the hands,
the humanoid arms and hands.
Mark of us creatures who stand upright.
With these arms we reach,
we lift,
we carry,
we hold.
We stretch forth our arm, we bend it.
We hold others to us,
body to body,
face to face.

As we reach with our arm our hand stretches forward,
the humanoid hand,
able to write, to grasp, to feel, to caress.
Four fingers and a thumb,
playing the music of the world:
Hands writing the wisdom of the world,
Hands molding the creation.
Hands touching others in love and sharing.

Wondrous arms with bends and angles,
wondrous hands with bends and angles.
The bent arm—the letter daled
the fingers and thumb—a daled
the bend of the fingers—a daled
shin and daled **ד**   shadd.

And finally, at the core,
a letter yod.

*A boy's yod is open, in front.*
*A girl's yod is hidden, in her midst.*
*The yod* י.
*Site of a joy not bounded by time,*
*site of a love that knows no seasons.*
*The yod of a human being:*
*future-creator,*
*pleasure-bringer,*
*binder of love.*
*A gift from God of God's own name,*
*for us to use in love of God.*


Shin, Daled, (ד), Yod,
Shaddai.
*The great Almighty of our ancestors*
*has sealed this divine name on our bodies.*
Shaddai.
*Every child comes with the name of God.*
*Blessed be the one who comes in the name of God.*    (Ps. 118:26)
*Blessed be the child,*
*Blessed be God.*
Shaddai.


# Rituals of Affirmation

The creation of a human being is a momentous process, and affirming it demands ritual expression. After their ambivalence has been resolved and their anxiety over early loss has subsided, then people are ready to affirm publicly their intention to have a child. The time will vary from person to person: one may be eager to affirm almost from the beginning, others only later, when chances for success are very great. For most people, the best time is during the fourth month when the fetus is fully formed and the chances for miscarriage are much less.

There are three elements in the affirmation of pregnancy: acceptance of responsibility for the baby to come, invocation of God's participation, and the initiation of a woman into a new state of existence. The two affirmation rituals that follow emphasize different aspects of this experience. The first is an initiation ritual or rite of passage: it brings the woman into a liminal period of anticipation and preparation during which the new being is not-quite-a-child and she is not-quite-a-new-mother. The second is a partnership ritual that binds the prospective parent(s) in a covenant with God in the creation and nurturing of the new human being. The first is a rite of passage loosely modeled on the Rite of Christian Initiation of Adults of the Catholic Church. The second is a covenantal ritual based on Jewish concepts and ceremonies. The final sacrament is, of course, birth itself.

# Rite of Passage

In many rites of passage, the transitional period is very short and is marked by a total withdrawal from society. However, pregnancy is more prolonged. It is similar to a catechumenate, in which the intended initiate has a lengthy period of preparation. The woman's public acceptance of her pregnancy is akin to the rite by which a would-be Catholic becomes a catechumen. The ritual has three participants: the pregnant woman, her sponsor, and the celebrants.

The pregnant woman steps up to announce her *intention* to

become a mother and her prayer that everything will go smoothly in the pregnancy. At this point she formally becomes a "catechumen," a "mother-in-waiting" consciously and publicly preparing herself for birth and motherhood. Each woman should have a sponsor who presents her to the celebrant and the community. This sponsor should be a woman who has recently given birth. A pregnant woman might choose a friend who has recently become a mother. If not, others in the community can match her with someone who has just had a baby. The sponsor then stays in contact with the woman during this next stage of pregnancy, acting as her supporter and her mentor. There is a dual purpose for this partnership: It gives the pregnant woman someone to whom she may turn, and, at the same time, gives the new mother a chance to debrief and to consolidate her own experiences.

The choice of celebrant depends on the community. If the ceremony is performed in the pregnant woman's home church, then the celebrant could be the pastor. The ceremony could also be held in a group of friends. In that case, the celebrant could be a respected member of that community, possibly an older woman.

The ritual consists of two parts: the invitation and the signing.

## THE INVITATION

CELEBRANT: *Are you ready to enter on this path to motherhood?*

PREGNANT WOMAN: *I am.*

CELEBRANT (TO SPONSOR AND ASSEMBLY): *Are you ready to help her achieve her goal?*

EVERYBODY: *We are.*

PREGNANT WOMAN:

*In the path of my God, I set upon this journey.*
*In the company of my Creator, I seek to create.*

*I do not know whether I will get there.*
*I cannot know what obstacles lie in my path.*
*I know not whether my efforts will bring life.*
*But I am ready to try.*

## THE SIGNING

The pregnant woman's friends form a circle around her and the celebrant. The celebrant draws a circle on the woman's forehead and says:

CELEBRANT: *For the fullness of spirit you bring to us,*
*and the fullness of the body you bring to the task,*
*toward the fulfillment of your task,*
*in the fullness of days,*
*I draw this circle.*
EVERYBODY: *May the circle be a circle of life.*

The celebrant continues drawing circles on parts of the woman's body and says at the appropriate times:

CELEBRANT: *I draw a circle on your ears:*
*May you hear the voice of God.*
EVERYBODY: *May the circle be a circle of life.*
CELEBRANT: *I draw a circle on your eyes:*
*May you see the light of God.*
EVERYBODY: *May the circle be a circle of life.*
CELEBRANT: *I draw a circle on your lips:*
*May you speak in the spirit of God.*
EVERYBODY: *May the circle be a circle of life.*
CELEBRANT: *I draw a circle on your stomach:*
*May you feel the Presence of God.*
EVERYBODY: *May the circle be a circle of life.*

THE PREGNANT WOMAN:
> May the circle be a harbinger
> of the roundness to come,
> of the unbroken ring of life,
> and the completion of the fruit of my body.

EVERYBODY: *Amen*.

CELEBRANT:
> God and Creator:
> You who created us in your likeness,
> guide with love the one who comes to you today,
> so that she may give thanks forever. *Amen*, Selah.

EVERYBODY: *Amen*, Selah.

# Covenant of Creation

The Biblical notion of "covenant" between God and humans helps us understand that the relationship of humans and God in the creation of new life is the relationship of partners. In their willingness to bear the child, the parents become God's "partners in the work of creation." This is a significant concept, for Judaism considers the work of God's creation to be unfinished, and it is part of humanity's task to continue this labor, to become *Shutafim lema'asey breshit*, "partners in the work of creation." One can become a partner liturgically, as the Talmud declares:

> *Everyone who prays on Friday night and says "[And the heavens and the earth] were finished," scripture considers to have become a partner of the Blessed Holy One in the works of creation.*

One can become a partner through social action, as the Talmud also states:

*Every judge who judges a righteous judgment even once Scripture considers to have become a partner to the Blessed Holy One in the works of creation.*

There is another, obvious way in which we can be partners of God in creation: by helping to create new lives. The *Iggeret Haqodesh,* a twelfth-century marriage manual, recognizes this distinctive feature of human sexuality:

*The union of a man and his wife is a mystery of the creation of the world and its population, for in it humanity becomes a partner of the Holy Blessed One in the works of Creation.*

The mother is a partner in creation throughout the stages of pregnancy, continually working with God to create the new life. In this ritual, the mother-to-be affirms this covenantal role and declares her willingness to be God's partner and to accept whatever hardships and sacrifices this deed might entail. She may be accompanied by her partner, too, who also professes willingness to affirm and support the pregnancy and the child to come. The ritual is written also to involve a celebrant and a community, for, even though the decision to bear children is a personal family choice, the birth of a child is a communal event. The community should affirm each couple's choice to have children, witness their acceptance of their duties, celebrate their decision, and offer communal support and encouragement for their endeavors. Every joyously accepted pregnancy sanctifies all of us.

# A Covenant Ceremony

THE MOTHER (WITH OR WITHOUT PARTNER):

> *I declare myself (We declare ourselves) fully ready to fulfill the commandment "Be fruitful and multiply" that God handed down to us on the day when God created us and on the day when God rescued us from the waters of the flood. And in order to fulfill this commandment, I (we) hereby come to enter the covenant which God has made with the daughters of Eve.*

THE MOTHER:

> *For Eve first recognized this bond of creation,*
>  *affirming it at the birth of her first son,*
> *when she stated:*
> "I have created a man with the Lord"    (Gen. 4:1)
> *God who creates us*
> *has created in woman*
> *the power to continue and participate*
> *in God's creations on earth.*
> *I come today to affirm this partnership with God:*

> *In my womb You form the child,*     (Ps. 139:13)
> *in my womb, I nourish it.*
> *There You form and number the limbs,*   (Ps. 139:16)
> *there I contain and protect them.*
> *You who can see the child in my depths,*  (Ps. 139:15)
> *I who can feel the kicks and the turns—*
> *Together we count the months,*
> *together we plan the future.*   (Jer. 1:5, Isa. 49:5)
> *Flesh of my flesh,*
> *form of Your form,*      (Gen. 1:26)

*another human upon the earth;*
*a home for God in this, our world.*

*Knowing that it is not easy to be partner to God,*
*knowing that it is hard to be*
*member to a covenant*
*I state my desire*
*to observe all the laws, commandments, and*
    *obligations*
*of this covenant.*
*As the mother of Samson before his birth,*    (Judg. 13:4–5)
*I, too, will refrain from drinking all wine, beer, or*
    *other alcohol,*
*and from eating impure foods.*
*I will not smoke, use drugs, or drink coffee or*
    *caffeine.*
*I will care for my body*
*and the life I shelter within me.*
*I declare that I will prepare to give my child*
*a faithful home in Israel,*
*and I will love this child with all my heart,*
*learning even as it grows within me,*
*the depths of mother-love.*

THE OTHER PARENT (IF PRESENT):
*In the months to come and the years to follow,*
*I will be mindful of the fact*
*that I, too, am a partner in this act of creation.*
*I will help in these months of her great effort,*
*and will do everything that I can*
*to enable her to observe these rules and obligations.*

*Together we will prepare our faithful home,*
*together we will welcome our baby,*

> together we will love, protect, instruct, and cherish
>     the child we are creating.

THE PARENTS:

> And now, You, for Your part:
> Pour Your spirit on our seed,
> your blessings on our offspring.                    (Isa. 44:3)
> Grant our child health and strength,
>     happiness and length of days.
> May the child grow
>     at peace with self and with the world.
> And let us continue to work together,
> we and You,
> to form a true righteous human,
> one who can walk with God,
> one who will say, "I am the Lord's"
> and carry proudly the name "Israel."              (Isa. 44:5)
> As we have entered this covenant,
> so may we be privileged
> to bring our child to a life of Torah, love and
>     righteous acts.
> And let us say Amen.

CONGREGATION: Amen.

The celebrant offers the following "personal prayer" (Mi Sheberach):

> May the one who blessed our ancestors
> Abraham, Isaac, and Jacob,
> Sarah, Rivkah, Rachel, Leah, Bilhah and Zilpah.
> Bless this woman _____ (and
>     _____) because they have
> entered this pact with our creator.

For this, may the Holy Blessed One
be full of mercy for her
to keep her safe, alive, healthy, and well.
And may God bring forth the child          (Job 10:18; Ps. 22:9–11)
      from her womb
at a good and propitious time.

For You are the one
who brings on labor and brings on birth.          (Isa. 66:9)

May it be Your wish
that her parents will be privileged
to raise children
to the Torah, the wedding canopy,
      and to a righteous life.

And let us say, Amen.

CONGREGATION: *Amen.*

*Congregation then sings:*
      May the Lord bless you from Zion.
      May you see the good of Jerusalem.
      May the Lord bless you all the days of your life,
      and may you see your children's children;
      Peace on Israel.          (Ps. 128:5–6)

# LOSS

Sometimes, tragically, the pregnancy ends suddenly, unbidden. Even the best intentions, the most fervent prayers, the best diet and medical care, the most heartfelt rituals cannot ensure a live birth. Despite our wishes, miscarriage is the normal outcome of many pregnancies. Miscarriage is a sad and significant event that demands its own rituals and liturgies. In their loss and sorrow, people must face this somber truth, and they must somehow find the courage to continue, to trust, and even to try again. They must express their dismay, their grief, and their anger at their inexplicable and irremediable loss:

> *Twice even the Temple was destroyed—*
> *the Temple, address of God,*
> *focus of prayer,*
> *seat of God's name,*
> *God's Presence,*
> *God's power.*

> *We loved the Temple.*
> *We came rejoicing*
> *and in sorrow.*
> *We came in feasting*
> *and in penitence,*
> *on festivals*
> *and sabbaths and feast days*
> *and no special days at all.*
> *We brought our sacrifices*
> *and our songs,*
> *the fruits of our labors.*

We loved the Temple
and the God whose Presence filled the Temple
and yet, the Temple was destroyed.

Was there something terribly wrong with the
        Temple?
Something that could not have been fixed
short of destruction?

There were worlds that God created and destroyed
before our world came to be.
What was wrong with them?
Was God practicing the art of creation
or whimsically testing the power to end?

Some are not meant to be.
Some disappear before they even arrive
What was wrong now?
Is this destruction a mercy?

Or is it You, God—
Has Your right arm withered?                    (Ps. 77:9–13)
Have You lost Your power?
Is all Your great and glorious might
lost in the battles of the past?

Or is it only in battle that we find Your presence?
In the hearts of men,
and not the wombs of women?

Yet I will recall the mighty deeds of God,
I will keep them before my eyes.
I recite them by day and by night.

# 5. MIDPASSAGE

The woman and her developing child set out on a journey. For the child, a steady voyage toward personhood, toward life. For the mother, a journey toward a new stage of life, a new existence. At first pregnancy, the woman takes a trip into mystery, a profound adventure into motherhood. Each later pregnancy brings her back to newness as she once again undergoes the transformations that turn her into a mother-of-newborn-infant. These journeys of motherhood are most rewarding to those who travel mindfully, reflecting on their path and affirming the changes that are taking place and the emotions they generate.

The first step of a journey is farewell. The voyager is leaving her old life and should take the time to consider what she is leaving forever, and what she is putting on indefinite hold. For some women, especially young first-time mothers, the losses entailed in becoming a mother are considerable— loss of childhood, of freedom from constraint, of financial independence—and midpassage can be a time of grieving for these losses and working through that grief. For a mother of older children, midpassage can be a journey of both loss and yearning as it brings her back to that bittersweet period of dependence that children spend their lives outgrowing.

The journey leads to new or renewed motherhood, and the months of pregnancy are a time to reflect on maternity, on the great mothers of the past, on one's own mother, on the life of mothers, and on the images and memories that have shaped our conception of motherhood. They are also a time to think about children, about their safe birth and our hopes for their lives.

This journey is intensely physical. It takes place in an ever-changing body that changes the way we interact with the world. As we think about the wonderful tasks that this body is performing, we cannot remain unaware of the many changes the body is undergoing and its dramatically new size and shape. Why is the body large? Why is it round? What does this roundness mean?

The months of midpassage are busy months. The pregnant woman focuses on her hopes for the child and her dread of misfortune; her anticipation of the child's future and her anxiety that not all will go well; her pride at creating a child and her lack of ease due to her ungraceful bulk; her joy at the coming birth and her fear of being prematurely joyful; her reaching for others and her focus on herself. In these months, the woman reflects on what is happening to her and becomes spiritually in tune with the newly developing other. As the body creates the child, the mind must form the mother.

## Following the Mother Line

We have been brought here by multimillennia of mothers: genealogical mothers, anthropological mothers, spiritual mothers, psychological mothers, divine mothers. It is time to remember the mothers, to study them, recall, record, and celebrate them.

The beginning of mother-memory may be a maternally focused genealogy. "I, daughter of woman, daughter of woman, daughter of woman." This genealogical chain celebrates the handing over of motherhood from generation to generation. Most links are biological, recording the transfer of genes from ovary to ovary. Some links are sociological, recording the handing down of motherhood and tradition by adoption rather than by parturition. My own chain is very short. The child of a family decimated by the holocaust, I have very few familial memories. Other women's chains are also too short. Even when families have not been destroyed by war and genocide, women's ability to trace their mothers is often very limited. Only recently have women even begun to try. My daughter will be able to trace one more generation than I can; her daughter, yet another. We must begin somewhere.

So we must each start with our own chain, short as it may be. At each pregnancy women can remember their mothers. And the mothers will become a living memory. Here is mine. I encourage you to make your own.


### THE CHAIN OF ME

*I am Tikva.*
*scholar, writer, teacher.*
*mother of Meira and Eitan.*
*daughter of Elyse,*
*ballet dancer, clothes designer*
*refugee from Paris,*
*mother of two.*

*Elyse is daughter of Helene*
*grande dame of Latvia*
*widowed young*
*refugee to Paris,*
*mother of four.*
*Helene, daughter of Sarah(?)*
*mother of fourteen.*

READER'S CHAIN

# Myth Mothers

Our mother figures are not only in our genes. Each of us lives in many families. We have our birth family tree, our family of friends and a family of the mind. In each of these it is important to trace the mother line. A pregnant woman might bring her mother-friends together and ask them all to speak about what they like about themselves as mothers and what they like about motherhood. Or she could speak to each one separately and record their replies in a mothering-booklet. Another activity would be to select some archetypical mothers from literature or films or television shows and articulate what she likes about each mother, thereby defining for herself what makes a good mother and identifying the qualities in herself that will make her a good mother. These women and these qualities should be honored by being written, thereby creating a moment of history and a document to remind the mother-to-be of the importance of her task.

The mother line reaches back to the primordial mothers, women who go inconceivably far back into the beginning of prehistory. These are women whom paleoanthropology has discovered in recent years, mothers we know only from their fossil skeletons. The earliest of these, known as "Lucy," lived three million years ago in Africa. She is the earliest full skeleton of a human being. In 1987, microbiology gave us another mother, one never expected, who lived shockingly few years ago. This woman, whom scientists call "Mitochondrial Eve," is said to have lived less than 200,000 years ago and to be the direct ancestress of all living humans. She is named after our mitochondria, little organelles within each cell in the human body. These organelles process our food, turning sugar into energy. The organelles are situated in the cytoplasm of the cell rather than the nucleus. There is no room for mitochondria in sperm, and as a result, the mitochondria of our bodies come only from our mothers' eggs. Our mitochondria would be genetically exactly the same as those of our mother, except for the fact that genes mutate over time. These mutations, the microbiologists tell us, occur at a fixed rate, and scientists can calibrate how long ago a family or group branched off by measuring the genetic variation between the members. They then calculate elapsed time according to this rate and produce the "microbiological clock."

By studying the DNA in the mitochondria of a wide sample of human beings, many microbiologists have concluded that all human beings alive today are descended from one woman who lived, most probably in Africa, less than 200,000 years ago. The genetic makeup of this woman gave her mito-chondria an edge in the production of energy, and therefore this woman's descendants have prospered and continue the maternal lineage through today. All other human families, de-scended from all other mothers, died out. This woman, who sounds more like a science-fiction character than a scientific discovery, was truly the "mother of us all."

In the Bible, the mother of us all is Eve, who gave mito-chondrial Eve her name. Mother Eve, the matriarchs Sarah, Rivka (Rebecca), Rachel and Leah, and Hannah and Mary, are the mythical mothers of our Western culture. These women enter our consciousness when we are still young and people the tales that shape our souls.

Eve has had a bad rap. Like mothers forever, she gave humanity our first taste of knowledge. Is this a tale of the "Fall" or the beginning of the ascent of humankind? Was Eve blame-worthy, or was she the first adventurer/discoverer? Each one of us must decide.

Genesis next names the mothers of Israel: Sarah, Rivka, Rachel, Leah. At first glance, it seems that homage to the matriarchs might be another example of praising the wives of famous men. But Sarah, Rivka, Rachel, and Leah are active mothers and shapers of Israel. They all show a choice for God, a taste for adventure, a willingness to explore. Tradition records and celebrates the merit of these women, as well as their status.

The motherhood of all these women needed God's partic-ular attention: we are told that "God took note of Sarah" (Gen. 21:1), that God listened on behalf of Rivka (Gen. 25:21), that God heard Leah (Gen. 30:17), and that God remembered Ra-chel and heard her (Gen. 30:22). Later Jewish women re-minded themselves of the great attention that God gave these matriarchs as they became mothers and prayed that they too would receive divine help.

Two mothers, Hannah in the Hebrew Bible and Mary in the New Testament, sang songs about themselves. In many respects, these two women are complements of each other. Both were mothers of men who shaped history. Hannah prayed for a child and was sent word that she would bear a son. Mary was told of her pregnancy without warning or request. Both responded to the announcement with songs of praise and thanksgiving. Hannah is remembered as the model of prayer that is answered, Mary for her consent to God's will.

## MOTHERS

Lucy.
From Africa.
Slight delicate woman, standing erect
three million years ago: mother in bone.


Eve,
unseen mother,
traced in our genes.
Borne in our cells, from mother to mother to mother,
her little organelles create the energy of life.
Unknown mother,
we carry your gift within us,
mother in protein, mother in cells.


Biblical Eve,
Mother of all living.
Lady of autonomy and disobedience,
lady of culture and wisdom.
You ate the knowledge—and shared it.

Yours was the knowledge and the struggle
and the glory and the pain.
We remember the one who created with God
mother of our triumph,
mother of our sorrows,
mother of life.

To Sarah, Rivka, Rachel, Leah,
servants of God and mothers of Israel,
women to whom God attended:

To the one who went with Abraham
on their journey to home and God.
God took note of you
spoke of you,
spoke to you.
So will I,
Sarah.

To the one who went again,
her own new journey
to the same destination,
the very same God.
You who chose adventure, chose life.
God listened for you,
Rivka.

To the two who went once more,
traveling with Jacob
to the same homeland,
choice of love.
Leah the less-loved
mother of many
God heard you

*God remembered and heard,*
*Leah and Rachel.*

*Sarah, Rivka, Rachel, Leah*
*the destiny of Israel lies with you.*
*May God who answered you our holy mothers*
*answer also me.*
*In your memory and your merit*
*may I remember God,*
*may God remember me.*
*Sarah Rivka Rachel Leah.*
*Mothers in the book*
*mothers of us all.*

*To Hannah and Mary,*
*whose horn was exalted,*
*who magnified the Lord.*
*Whose songs ring forever.*
*The one who asked for a child,*
*the one who received one unbidden.*
*Two mothers who waited,*
*two mothers who knew.*
*mothers of leaders,*
*of godly men.*
*mothers of memory*
*mothers of song.*

*I sing to all the mothers of my myths,*
*to all the mothers of my past.*
*I respond to the mother of my genes,*
*and the mothers of my soul.*
*I remember the mothers-in-bone*
*and the mothers-in-song.*
*I am conscious of all who came before me,*

*and to all I say,*
*"God pray I join you!*
*I too would be mother in genes,*
*in flesh, in bone, in love.*
*With the mothers from the past,*
*let me be mother of tomorrow."*

# Mothers Divine

Beyond all these celebrated human mothers lies the archetype of motherhood herself, the divine mother. These divine beings —the great Goddess of Paleolithic times, the mother-goddess of ancient mythology, the mother-god of monotheism—serve as emblems of the divinity of motherhood.

Ancient Paleolithic peoples made statues and drawings of a primordial great goddess-mother. The most famous of these, the Venus of Willendorf, typifies this woman-figure. Large droopy breasts, prominent stomach and buttocks, large thighs: this is the womanhood that we have learned to scorn, woman built for nurture and comfort and solidity. To very ancient people, this is the womanhood that typified life: creator of life, nourisher of the living, sustainer of life. The bliss of the womb and the breast are captured in this pillowed body.

By the neolithic domestication of animals, the need for a male in the herd was well understood. In literate societies, mother-goddess is joined by father-god as the great creator of humankind. In the Bible, the two have been fused. The divine mother is very much present in the Bible as God's role in creation is stressed, from the creation of the first humans,

Adam and Eve, to the conception of Israel's ancestors to the creation of each human being. It is God who forms the child in the womb of its mother, God who supervises and protects it there and may determine its destiny, God who supervises the birth. The functions of the mother-goddess have not been forgotten; they have been absorbed into the one deity who is both god and goddess.

## PRIMORDIAL MOTHER

*Great Mother.*
*Fat mother.*
*Mother with large abundant breasts,*
*Mother with ample pillow stomach,*
*Mother with hips and spreading thighs,*
*Mother there,*
*Mother solid.*

*I see your image in my memory:*
*No girl-come-play woman,*
*no catch-me-if-you-can woman,*
*no you've-come-a-long-way-*
*go-for-the-burn-*
*you're-not-getting-older-you're-getting-better-*
*eternal youth-*
*virgin mother-*
*mamita-Lolita woman.*
*Mother.*
*Solid, substantial*
*giant-goddess mother.*
*mother of once,*
*mother of stone.*

## MAMI CREATES HUMANKIND

———————— ∞ ————————

According to a Babylonian myth, this story of the creation of humankind should be told at each birth:

> (The story begins with a dilemma: the gods, who have to work to grow their food, find the work laborious and wish to create a worker to feed them. They call in the mother-goddess, and ask her to create humankind. When she demands the god Enki's participation, he sets up a purifying bath, slaughters a minor god who has the rationality that humanity will need, and she mixes the clay with the blood of this god.)

> *Mami opened her mouth and said to the great gods,*
> *"You commanded me a task—I complete it.*
> *You slaughtered a god with his sense—*
> *I remove your heavy labor,*
> *and place your labor-basket on humankind.*
> *You called for humankind:*
> *I have unloosened your yoke, have established freedom."*

> *They heard this speech of hers,*
> *ran and kissed her feet.*
> *"Formerly we called you 'Mami'*
> *Now let your name be 'mistress of all the gods.' "*

> *They entered the house of destiny,*
> *Prince Ea and wise Mami.*
> *With the birth goddesses assembled,*
> *He trod the clay in her presence.*
> *She recited the incantation again and again . . .*

*The womb goddesses were assembled.*
*Nintu was seated . . .*
*She counted the months.*
*At the destined time, they called the tenth month.*
*The tenth month came, the end of the period opened the womb.*
*Her face was beaming, joyful.*
*Her head covered,*
*she performed the midwifery . . .*

*"I have created, my hands have done it."*
*Let the midwife rejoice in the sacral house . . .*
*Praise the birth goddess, praise Kesh!*

# Mother to Mother

The God of the Bible cares for Israel as a nurturing parent—as a mother and a father. We who embark on parenthood, on pregnancy and then on nurturance, are following in the footsteps of God, are acting in the highest tradition of *imitatio dei,* the copying of God. So, too, God is our fellow mother, who can understand what we endure and what we attempt.

*When you were pregnant with Israel, Lord*
*——did your ankles swell?*
*——did your fingers tingle and droop?*
*Did you spend your time waiting, marking time,*
*and doing infinite chores?*

*After you announced the birth of the nation,* (Gen. 15:13–15)
*knowing it would be long, three generations*
*long,*

*till the birth of the people on its land—*
*After you announced this birth, Lord—*
    *did you sit counting the days and the years?*
*Did you plan how you would raise Ephraim,*
    *your darling child?* (Jer. 31:20)
    *how you would call him from Egypt,*
    *draw him with cords of love?* (Hos. 11:1)
*Did you count the days*
    *till you could teach him to walk?* (Hos. 11:13)
    *till you could bend down and feed him each*
        *morsel?* (Hos. 11:4)
*When you carried Israel in your womb, O Lord,*
*did you think how you would nurture forever,*
    *how you would carry him till old-age?* (Isa. 46:3–4)
*Did you plan every moment of his upbringing,*
    *dreaming of the perfect child?*
*Or were you very busy, Lord,*
    *planning universes,*
    *setting up laws,*
    *organizing history?*

# Mother-Woman

There is a distinct character to the state of pregnancy, a special status of all pregnant women. During this period the pregnant woman enters a unique time, touched by divinity, in which she keeps company with the force that creates us all.

*When I see women now—*
*sometimes I see wombs.*
    *not vaginas-tits-and-ass,*

but wombs.
*Have you borne children?*
*Are you bearing now?*

*Not all women are mothers:*
*Some women cannot,*
*some will not,*
*and some never get the chance.*
*Biology is not destiny,*
*women are not nature,*
*women who do not mother are still women.*
*A woman who does not mother is not less than a man.*

*But—I am afraid to say this aloud:*
*A woman who gives birth is more.*
*Maybe only for that period from conception to birth,*
*a woman who gives birth is more.*
*Touched by sacred mission,*
*containing magic action,*
*channeling the destiny of all,*
*redoing creation,*
*and, maybe, even altering it.*

*I am afraid to say this aloud:*
*Perhaps I should shout it from rooftops.*

### *WOMAN CAN BE MOTHER*
### *MOTHER CAN BE CREATOR*

*But maybe it is enough to whisper it.*
*Powerful whisper,*
*secret sigh of a sacred society.*

*Soon I will be an ordinary person again,*
*with all the cares and joys of men and women,*
*working and loving and seeking God.*
*Now is my chance to feel myself touched by divinity,*
*tapped for a sacred role.*
*Now is my hour to add to the kingdom,*
*share in the power,*
*rejoice in the glory.*
*To partake for a moment in foreverness,*
*and spend a little eon in the One.*

# Growth

Pregnancy is accompanied by a drastic change in shape and weight. Women gain at least a quarter and frequently over a third of their prepregnancy body weight. This brings physical distress to legs, feet, and back. It can also bring psychological stress. Women who have spent time and energy trying to stay concave now become hugely convex. The pregnant woman grows larger, ever larger, ever rounder. In our culture, obsessed with standards of "looking good" and enamored of extreme thinness, women can have a hard time coming to terms with their increasing bulk.

The largeness of pregnancy cannot be ignored: not by the woman, who copes daily with its consequences; and not by those around her, who are forced by her size to take note of her pregnancy. The sheer size of pregnancy impresses itself upon our consciousness. We can be unaware of or willfully ignore the pregnancy of many animals, but no one can miss the pregnancy of a woman. Her size is a signpost that something is happening, something that demands our attention.

Inside, a human being is growing. The birth of all beings is a joyous continuation of nature. A human being is even more: a sacred creation in the image of God. Every human being contains the divine image, the divine spark and the divine presence. A woman forming a human being is creating a place for God's presence in this world, birthing a bit of divinity. The largeness of the pregnant woman cries out to us: look, behold! a human being.

## BEHOLD THE HUMAN (John 19:15)

*I am growing larger.*
    *My arms are thicker,*
    *my hips have spread.*
    *Most of all, my front has extended.*
*It is harder for my legs to carry me,*
*my back aches with the strain.*

*You are not this big, my tiny mite.*
*Even born you will be small.*
*While I grow larger and larger,*
*rounder and rounder,*
*¹/₂ lb a week, a pound a week, two pounds a week.*

*A cat, who gives birth to five or six, stays smoothly sleek,*
*maybe a little fatter, a little slower,*
*nothing that you would notice.*
*A horse, whose colt is born big and able to stand,*
*still doesn't gain ¹/₃ of her weight.*

*But I am already growing, changing my shape and my clothes.*
*Look at me! my body says.*
*Pay attention!*

*I will get larger and larger*
*till your eyes—and all eyes—cannot fail to see.*
*This is not the birth of a cat*
*nor of a mouse, or a dog*
*or even a dolphin.*

*Ecce homo!*
*I am growing a human.*
*With blood and matter*
*—and divinity.*
*This tiny being within me will someday be a person.*
*A spirit who loves and thinks,*
*and lives in the image of God.*

*Once, they say, there was a theotokos,*
*woman-give-birth-to-God,*
*creating and nurturing and carrying and forming and nourishing*
*the One who creates and nurtures.*
*Woman who sheltered the sheltering Presence*
*woman who formed the Former.*

*Every child is an incarnation*
*of soul, of spirit, of love.*
*Every child shelters the spark,*
*embodies the image,*
*gives home to the Presence.*
*Every child manifests the being of God,*
*does God's work on earth.*

*I look at this belly,*
*grown so enormous:*
*my body has extended beyond my own being.*
*It forms flesh into more-than-flesh,*
*creates life into the future.*

*Ecce homo!*
*Behold the human!*
*I too am mother-of-divine.*

# Round Is the Belly, Round is the World

The belly of a pregnant woman is not only large, it is round. Round, like the globe; round like a ring. A ring that has no beginning and no end, symbol of eternity, sign of our weddings. A pregnancy has a beginning—conception—and an end—childbirth. Nevertheless, a pregnancy is round, as the roundness can symbolize the unending cycle of human existence. Each individual pregnancy may have a beginning and an end, but pregnancy is the link to our future, and childbirth is the moment when our past, present, and future meet. The roundness of pregnancy can serve to make us mindful that procreation is the way that we create our own futures, and birth is the moment when we assure the life of our families, our society, our species.

## ROUND

*The snake puts its tail in its mouth and bites.*
*A ring, eternity.*
*Ouroboros.*
*Memory of mother's womb surrounding us,*
*reflection of the wheel of time,*
*curve of the heavens around us.*

Dragon circling the earth,
container, protector, mother.


I eat an egg in the springtime:
Haman's egg, Easter egg,
Passover egg that has no name.
I celebrate the regrowth of life.
New beginnings.
Chicks and lambs, bunnies
and eggs.
The seasons turn around.
Another spring,
life goes on.


I eat an apple in the fall,
round fruit of autumn,
sweetened with honey.
Sweet for a sweet year, round for a new year.
the seasons turn.
Another autumn:
life goes on.


I bake my autumn bread a round,
round and whole, swelling to the top:
round for the new year,
sweetened with honey.
Another autumn, another year.
Around and around
the round of life.


I give my love a ring that has no end.
A ring when it's rolling, it has no end.

*My life starts and will end,*
*but the circle of life goes on.*

*The earth turns, the seasons turn,*
*the chain of being spirals on.*
*My womb is now a rolling circle*
*of life-no-end,*
*of life goes on.*

# Jerusalem, Mountains Surround Her

The circle contains and protects. People gather around in a circle; they circle their wagons in the field. Circles of people, circles of walls, circles of cities. Rome was built in a circle, as was Jerusalem. The womb of a woman is a human Jerusalem. Like the temple, it is purified by blood; God guards its gates, protecting the child within. As a sacred precinct, it contains the divine Presence. And as pregnancy goes on, the woman looks ever more like the city of Jerusalem and the mountains that surround her.

> *Yerušalayim, harim saviv lah,*
> *vaYHWH saviv le'amo me'ata we'ad 'olam.*
> Jerusalem, mountains surround her,
> and God surrounds the people
> from now until forever.—(Ps. 125:2)

*I am become like a mountain*
*swelling,*
*reaching into the earth,*
*rising to the sky.*

*and you, within, are Jerusalem,*
*place where the people live,* (Isa. 10:24)
*place where God resides.* (Ps. 9:12)
*I am become like Jerusalem,*
*round walls encircling life,*
*domes lifting their heads,*
*and you within are Mount Zion,* (Ps. 9:12)
*dwelling place of God,*
*resting place for Shekhinah.*

*I am indeed Mount Zion,*
*mountain inside the city,*
*and you within me are the Temple*
*which contains the Holy of Holies*
*in which lives the Presence.*

*I am mother-Zion,*
*mother of her inhabitants,*
*and great in my midst is the Holy One of Israel.* (Isa. 12:6)
*The Lord is within me,*
*forming the life,*
*creating the life,*
*and resting within.*
*And the Lord surrounds me,*
*encircling the people,*
*protecting and enveloping*
*the me who protects,*
*the me that encircles.*

*I who am encircled by God,*
*encircle you.*
*I surround the holy*

*and am surrounded by it.*
*God within and God without—*
*the mountain of me is the mountain of Yah.*

# The Cosmic Body

The world itself is round. The globe that we stand on is round and it revolves around itself, turning in its own circle as it travels in its circle around the sun. The ancients didn't know our astronomy, but their world also was round: when the earth beneath is our base, then the skies above form a round vault from horizon to horizon, just like a pregnant woman lying on her back.

*I am the curve of the universe.*
*My back is the earth*
       *stretched over the nothingness*         (Job 26:7)
    *floating on the cosmic sea.*         (Exod. 20:4)
*My pregnant stomach*
    *is the great vault of the heavens,*
    *stretched out like a tent*         (Isa. 41:22)
*And within—a universe of life.*

# World of the Womb

When we see the womb as the vault of the heavens, then we realize that the vault of the heavens may also be a womb, the womb of God.

*Hayoshev al hug ha'arets*
*veyoshveha kahagavim.*
God sits on the Circle of the Earth
and we appear as grasshoppers. (Isa. 40:22)

*I fold my hands on the circle of my stomach*
*and I am outside it.*
*Tiny creature hidden within—*
*My eye cannot see you.*
*My will cannot control you.*
*But I feel your presence,*
*and I note your being,*
*and I wish you all blessings,*
*and I love you.*

*Inside the circle of the earth we move,*
*beings colliding, uniting, apart.*
*Thinking our thoughts,*
*doing our deeds.*

*Outside our view,*
*surrounding us,*
*is God.*
*The one who contains,*
*who nourishes,*
*and lets us be.*

*We live in the womb of God.*

# La Ronde

The fertilized egg is round; the globe is round; the vault of the heavens is round. The shape keeps reappearing in nature, from the smallest to the largest element, from the nucleus of an atom to the sun and a galaxy and a spiral nebula. The sphere is not hard-edged: the nucleus of the atom is surrounded by an electron cloud; the earth has its clouds, the sun its corona, and the spiral nebula its aura. Like a fractal shape in geometry, the cosmic pattern of the misty circle repeats throughout nature on every scale. The *Zohar*, a thirteenth-century Jewish mystical book, sees this pattern in time. At the first moment in time, the infinite began to emerge into a finite world. At this primal moment, there appeared a *qutra' degulma' na'if be'azaqa*, "misty matter set in a circle." In the next step, God contracts, leaving some empty space that the world can fill—exactly as does the fertilized egg, which gets hollow as soon as it embeds in the womb, leaving an empty space for differentiation. Somehow the mystics, looking inward, divine the inner shape and dynamics of creation.

## CIRCLES UPON CIRCLES

*At the primal moment,*
*suddenly,*
qutra' degulma' na'if be'azaqa
*misty matter set in a circle.*

*At our first moment,*
*we are set in a circle*
*mists swirling, connecting;*
*then dividing,*

*segmenting,*
*traveling,*
*coming to the womb,*
*Enclosed in the primal circle,*
*exploding within.*

*Into my womb comes the embryo:*
*circles within circles,*
*embryos within womb*
*wombs within women*
*women within worlds*
*worlds within galaxies*

*circles within circles*
*wheels within wheels*
*mists of matter,*
*set in a circle*

qutra' degulma' na'if be'azaqa.

# Mandala

The circle or sphere draws our attention inward. Each point on the perimeter is equidistant from the center; each point pulls toward the center. We gaze into a crystal ball, we stare enrapt at a globe of the world, and we draw circles as an aid to meditation. These are called mandalas, a Sanskrit word for circle. From the rose windows of Gothic cathedrals to the drawings of the East, the mandala circle focuses our attention inward, to the energy of creation and the unity of all. The round belly of the pregnant woman is a mandala. Through it, we focus our attention inward to the life inside, and then even farther inward to the center of our self and eternity beyond.

> In good mystic's fashion I will contemplate my navel.
> My navel has grown large
> and open and deep.
> It leads me inward.
> My stomach grows large and round,
> like a circle drawn for meditation,
> my own mandala.

> I will contemplate my navel,
> meditate on my mandala.
> My flesh grows transparent, and I can see inside.
> Inside I see a tree, growing inward
> flowering in another navel
> "umbilicus" of my child.
> The tree pulses with life and blood
> bringing nourishment to the life within.

> At the end of the tree, the amnion,
> beautiful ball, corona of loveliness.
> Little spaceship that holds the growing being.
> Little voyager from eternity,
> from the single cell,
> ground of all being.

> Star voyager of the inner heavens,
> visitor from the beginning of time,
> time-traveler from past to future.
> Child of the eons of humankind,
> child to me.

## TO THE CHILD

*There was a time when I was like you.*
*Unformed.*
*Flesh in the making,*
*bones in the forming.*

*Now I give praise, for I am awesomely, wondrously made:*
*my soul knows it well.*
*Like you, I was shaped in a hidden place,*
*the womb of my mother,*
*the recesses of the earth.*

*Only God saw my unformed limbs*
*as they grew and knit together.*
*Yet slowly they formed, every one of them,*
*till I could be born.*

*I can not see you,*
*as my mother could not see me,*
*I cannot not see or control your forming.*
*But I give praise, for I am awesomely, wondrously made:*
*may you be too.*

*May God bestow on you life and care*
*and Providence watch over your spirit.* *

* This poem is based on Psalm 139:13–15, and the last two lines are from Job 10:8f.

# The Child to Come

Wonder at the process accompanies reveries about the baby. What will the child be like? Will it be a boy or a girl? Will it be a doctor or a lawyer or a carpenter or an artist? Will it play baseball or basketball or do karate or dance? Will it be nice or smart or cute or funny? Sometimes afraid to think such thoughts, pregnant women say, "As long as it's healthy!" Anxious not to ask too much aloud, women say, "May it live." And still, we dream . . .

Bela Yudita Coen's prayer book has a prayer for Italian Jewish women to add to their regular prayers every day throughout pregnancy. In this prayer, the mother-to-be prays for her ideal child to have wisdom, righteousness, piety, and success:

> *Be Gracious unto me*
> > *that the embryo inside me be not a sandal.*
> *May the embryo inside me*
> > *be righteous, upright and proper,*
> > *to stand before you in*
> > > *its wisdom and Torah and good deeds.*
> *May the child*
> > *be ready all its days for your worship and awe.*
> *May the child*
> > *be beloved and graceful*
> > *in the eyes of all above and below.*
> *Make for this child*
> > *organs flowing with Torah*
> > *as you made for Abraham, your cherished one.*
> *May the child be born at an auspicious hour*
> > *that it may have strength and might to worship you*

*and that it may have prosperity*
    *so that it may never depend on the gifts or loans of*
        *others.*

In an early Old Yiddish pregnancy petition, the mother is more detailed in her description and more specific in her requests:

*May the fruit in my body*
    *have no problems while I carry it.*
*May you open the doors and angles of my womb*
    *so that the child comes out as quickly*
        *as a hen lays an egg.*
*May it have no lack in all its 248 parts.*

*I pray you, If the child is a boy:*
*May it have a pure soul from the male world*
    *so that it can master your holy Torah*
    *and be smart and have an understanding heart.*
*May he be neither too light nor too dark,*
    *not too smart nor too foolish,*
    *but medium*
    *and may he find favor in the eyes of God and people.*
*May he have all the good qualities and virtues*
    *so that he can serve you*
    *with all his heart and body,*
    *his wealth and love and awe.*
*May he have long life in this world,*
    *a life spent seeking Torah and commandments,*
    *a good heart to do justice and good deeds.*
*May everything he does in his life,*
    *whether in spiritual matters or worldly matters*
    *be done for the sake of Heaven.*

*And if the fruit in my body is a daughter, I pray you:*
*Give her a pure soul*
    *that she should serve your holy name for the sake of Heaven.*
*May she have no lack in all her parts,*
*May she be pretty in form*
*and may she have all the good attributes.*

*May she know*
    *what a proper daughter of Israel*
    *should know about Jewish matters,*
    *to hear and read and write*
    *and to know all the crafts that women know.*
*May she be pious and gracious*
    *and do good deeds*
    *and do all the commandments that women have.*


## MY PETITION

These early-modern Jewish petitions stress piety and knowledge in children. They also assume differences between boys and girls. Today, each mother's petition should reflect her own values. This is a time to think about your prayer and to consider the characteristics that you consider ideal. Do you want a patient child? A funny one? A healthy one? A pious one? A sensitive one? Our wishes may not come true, our prayers are not always answered, our children have their own ideas about what they want to be. Despite this, it is important for us to identify the qualities that we value, and to image the characteristics that we want our children to have. You might insert your petition in this prayer:

*May the Child that I bear within me be well.*
*May the child that I bear with me be:*

*May the child be born easily and at the right time.*
*May the child that I bear with me be.*

# 6. DANGER AND DREAD

The last trimester is a time of waiting. The child is now fully formed and viable. Every day adds to its strength and health, and the chances of a successful pregnancy are very high. Thoughts turn increasingly to the birth, in both anticipation and anxiety. When will the child be born? Will it be healthy? As the hour approaches, it is important to acknowledge and confront fears as well as hopes, to express the terror that women may experience for their children and themselves.

## The Demon

Ever since Babylon, people have depicted these fears in the form of a dread demon whose job it is to snatch away the children. In Babylon this demon was called Lamashtu. She is not the devil, not a Babylonian personification of evil, neither the equivalent of Satan nor his daughter. She is, rather the wild daughter of An, the father of the gods. She has been given a dreadful job to do, for she must cause miscarriage, stillbirth, and perinatal death.

The story of the childsnatcher's beginning is told in the *Atrahasis Epic:* We pick up the story after humans have been created.

> (The creation of humanity has gone awry. There are too many people, making too much noise. The gods bring first plague, then drought and famine. But these are only temporary remedies, and the gods vote to bring a flood to end the problem once and for all.
>
> One god, Enki-Ea, saves Atrahasis and, through him, humankind. Then, after the flood, Ea introduces permanent population controls:)

*Let there be among the peoples a third class of people:*
    *women who bear and women who do not bear.*
*Let there be the Pashittu ("snatcher") demon*
    *to take away the child from the mother who bore it.*
*Let there be Entu-women, Ugbabtu women and Igitsitu women.*
*Let them be taboo and so stop childbirth.*

This childsnatcher, the Pashittu, is elsewhere known as Lamashtu, a fierce wild demon who devours children. This myth shows that she is part of the gods' design for the universe, an improvement in the creation of humanity who enables human life to continue by preventing overpopulation. The tragedy of an infant's death is, when all is said and done, part of the divine system that enables all life to live.

Nevertheless, no one wants to be the one whose child dies for the good of humanity. Every family in ancient Mesopotamia sought to protect its baby from becoming the Pashittu demon's victim. Every family would utter incantations against the demon, hang barriers against her, and perform protective rituals. These rituals, incantations, and amulets were all used to fight Lamashtu, to keep her away and make her impotent. One very common type of amulet is very small, with one ten-line inscription. These amulets were probably intended to be worn.

### LAMASHTU, DAUGHTER OF AN

*Lamashtu, daughter of An*
*whom the gods call by name,*
*Inanna, the heroine of the mistresses,*
*she who fetters the dangerous asakku,*
*important alu-demon of humanity.*
*Exceedingly great lamaštu,*
*do not approach this person!*
*Be adjured by heaven,*
*be adjured by earth!*

Many of the Lamashtu incantations are longer and describe the appearance and activities of both the demon and those who combat her. The following incantation emphasizes her noble heritage. She does not come from some nongodly realm. On the contrary, she is the daughter of the heaven god Anu, who is the father of the gods, and of the mother-goddess Aruru, the mother of both gods and humans. The incantation relates how her parents are distraught at her activities. They are unwilling to let her destroy their human creatures, but they also do not want to destroy her. They devise a plan to keep her away from human children:

## LAMASHTU

*A charm:*

*I am the daughter of the heavenly Anu.*
*Furious am I,*
    *impetuous,*
    *and awesomely bright.*

*Into a house I enter,*
    *out of a house I go:*
*"Bring me your sons,*
    *let me suckle them—*
*into the mouths of your daughters*
    *let me place my breast."*

*Anu heard and cried.*
*The tears of Aruru, mistress of the gods, began to flow.*
*"How can we destroy that which we have created,*
    *and let the wind carry away*
    *what we have brought into being?"*

*Let it take her to the ocean,*
    *the edge of the mountain.*
*Bind her side with a palm branch.*
*Because a dead person has no life,*
    *a miscarried fetus does not suckle*
        *its mother's milk.*

*Let the daughter of Anu go up to the heavens like smoke,*
*may she not come down.*

There are quite a few Lamashtu incantations, which the Babylonians themselves collected into an organized series for study and reference. I have compiled the following poem from several of these incantations:

### THE DAUGHTER OF AN

*Powerful is the daughter of An.*
*She who torments little babies—*
*like a net is her hand.*

*She, the fierce one,*
*the one who rages, punishes and snatches,*
*the fleet one who carries away—*
*she is the daughter of An.*

*Furious, impetuous, awesomely bright,*
*a very she-wolf—*
*she is the daughter of An.*

*She rises:*
*her hair hangs loose,*
*her loins are unclothed,*
*her hands are covered with blood and flesh.*

*Through the window she enters,*
*she glides like a snake.*
*At her will she enters a house;*
*at her will, she exits.*

*"Bring me your sons that I may suckle them;*
*into the mouths of your daughters, I place my breast."*

*She strikes the womb of the almost-delivered;*
*she takes away the child of the pregnant woman.*
*She makes them suck.*
*She lets them be*
    *and goes on her way.*

*I adjure you*
*that you come not into this house,*
*that you sit not in the seat in which I sit,*
*that the baby I bring to my embrace you take not into your own.*
*I adjure you*
    *by An your father,*
    *by Antum your mother,*
    *by Ea who made your name.*

The woman is not alone in her battle against Lamashtu. She has the aid of her family and community, who actively help with rituals, incantations, and amulets. These invoke the assistance of other members of the spirit world in this struggle. The welfare of pregnant and birthing women and of unborn and young babies depends on keeping Lamashtu away and supernatural aid is solicited. One of the more elaborate Lamashtu amulets is a large plaque that is topped by the head of Pazuzu, a mighty figure in Babylonian demonology. Pazuzu is a fearsome demon who himself can cause disease and distress. Here he is enlisted in the aid of the woman and child: his image is expected to frighten Lamashtu away.

On this amulet, the help is demonic. In the incantation above on p. 105 the parental pair Anu and Aruru try to control Lamashtu. In other incantations, the god Asarluhi comes to the aid of laboring women and other people in distress.

These concepts of the childsnatcher and her supernatural opponents outlived the Babylonians. *The Testament of Solomon,* an apocryphal work written in the first or second century C.E., has the woman in labor wear an amulet that invokes the aid of the angel Raphael against the childsnatcher Obizuth. King Solomon is speaking:

*There came before me a spirit in woman's form*
*that had a head without any limbs,*
*and her hair was disheveled. . . .*
*"I am called among men Obizuth,*
*By night I sleep not,*
*but go my rounds over all the world*
*and visit women in childbirth.*
*Divining the hour I take my stand,*
*and if I am lucky, I strangle the child.*
*But if not, I retire to another place,*
*for I cannot a single night retire unsuccessful.*

*I am a fierce spirit*
*of myriad names and many shapes.*
*And now hither, now thither I roam. . . .*
*I have no work other than the destruction of children,*
*making their ears to be deaf*
*and working evil to their eyes*
*and binding their mouths with a bond,*
*and ruining their minds,*
*and paining their bodies."*

*I, Solomon, heard this.*
*I marvelled at her appearance*
*for I beheld her body to be in darkness.*
*But her glance was altogether bright and cheery*
*and her voice was very clear as it came to me.*

I cunningly said,
"Tell me by what angel you are frustrated, O Evil Spirit?"
She answered me,
"By the angel of God called Afarof,
which is interpreted Raphael,
by whom I am frustrated now and for all time.
His name, if anyone know it,
write the same on a woman in childbirth,
then I shall not be able to enter her.
Of this name, the number is 640."

# The Childsnatcher's Names

Later amulets are designed to be hung in the room from late pregnancy until after mother and child are past immediate danger. Sometimes they record the secret names of the child-snatcher, who, like Rumpelstiltskin, can be thwarted by the use of her names. In Greek Christianity, the abominable child-snatcher is called Ghyllou. She reveals her twelve and a half names. Some names can be traced to their meanings, others are not so transparent:

"My first and special name is called Ghyllou:
the second Amorphous;
the third Abyzou;
the fourth Karkhous;
the fifth Brianē;
the sixth Bardellous;
the seventh Aigyptianē;
the eighth Barna;

*the ninth Kharkhanistrea;*
*the tenth Adikia;*
*( . . . ) the twelfth Myia;*
*the half Petomene."*

Other amulets have different names.

The name-amulets have a very long history. Sometimes the demon meets the archangel Michael and reveals her names. In Arabic tradition, the protagonists are King Solomon and the Karina. In Jewish tradition the demon is called Lilith, and the prophet Elijah meets her and asks her where she is going. She answers, "I am going to the house of the birthing woman. I am going to give her the sleep of death and to take the child born to her and suck its blood and suck its marrow and sign its flesh." Elijah curses her that she will become silent and still as a stone. She begs to be released from this curse and gives her names: wherever she sees them, she will leave.

When these stories and names were written on large amulets and hung on the walls, those in the room were reminded both of danger and of the help coming to fight the danger.

## Three Against the Childsnatcher

Another long-lived incantation against the childsnatcher takes the form of a historiola (a magic story) about three helpers who are appointed to protect the mother against the demon. The earliest example of this story comes from Israel in the fifth to sixth centuries C.E. The text is written on a thin silver sheet which is rolled up to be worn as an amulet. The Aramaic text inscribed on the sheet tells about Smamit, whose children had all been killed by Sideros. When Smamit again becomes pregnant, she flees. Three helpers, Swny, Swswny, and Snygly, come to see her, but when she opens her door, Sideros enters her house and kills the newborn. She cries, the fiend flees, and the helpers chase him and catch him in the middle of the sea. They are about to kill him when he swears that whenever the names Swny, Swswny and Snygly are mentioned, he will not kill the amulet maker's client and her child.

This story has an incredibly long history, appearing on amulets from Ethiopia to Romania, from ancient to modern times. Sideros, who is male, is usually replaced by the female child-snatching demon, but the story can always be recognized by the three avengers. Medieval Greek amulets tell of Meletine. She gave birth to six children, and the abominable Ghyllou carried them off. Meletine tried to hide in a tower for her next birth, but when she opened the door for her brothers, Saints Sisinios, Sinēs, and Sēnodōros, Ghyllou came in as a fly on their horses and killed the child. Empowered by an angel, they pursued her into the sea and overtook her. When they flogged her, she swore "by the disc of the sun and the horn of the moon that wherever your name is written and your association is known, and my twelve and a half names, I shall not dare approach that house but shall keep away from that house to a distance of three miles," and she told them her names.

The most famous of these demons is Lilith, who appears in medieval Jewish folklore. The three who thwart her are Sanvai, Sansanvai and Semongolof. Their story is told in a collection of fantastic tales, the Alpha-bet of Ben Sira, which was probably composed in Baghdad in the eighth or ninth century and is found in many European manuscripts beginning in the eleventh century.

Ben Sira was a wondrous sage at the court of King Nebuchadnezzar. When the king's infant son fell ill, Nebuchadnezzar asked Ben Sira, "Why do eight-day-old infants die?" and Ben Sira answered, "Lilith kills them." Nebuchadnezzar then ordered Ben Sira to heal him. Ben Sira wrote an amulet and inscribed the angels Sanvai, Sansanvai, and Semongolof by their names, their forms, their limbs, and their seals. When the king asked who they were, Ben Sira answered, "Angels" and told the following story:

### BEN SIRA'S STORY OF LILITH

*When God created Adam and saw that he was alone*
*God made a woman from the ground like him,*
*called her Lilith*
*and brought her to Adam.*

*Immediately they began to quarrel.*
*He said: "You lie underneath,"*
*and she said, "You lie underneath"*
*and they didn't listen to each other.*

*When Lilith saw this,*
*she pronounced the ineffable name,*
*rose into the air and fled.*

*Adam prayed before his maker, saying*
*"Master of the Universe,*
*the woman you gave me has already fled."*

*The Holy Blessed one sent these three angels.*
*God told them: "Bring back Lilith.*
*If she wants to come, she will come,*
 *but you may not bring her against her will."*

The three angels went
    and caught up to her in the sea
at the place where the Egyptians were destined to die.
There they grabbed her and said,
    "If you come with us, good,
    and if not, we will drown you in the sea."

She answered,
"Oh, my friends, I know by myself:
the Holy Blessed One created me
    to injure infants when they are eight days old.
From the day that he is born until eight days
I have power over him
and from eight days on I have no power over a boy child;
over a girl I have power twelve days."

They wouldn't leave her be until she swore to them by God:
        "Wherever I see you or your names
            on an amulet,
        I will have no power over that infant."
Straightaway they left her.

She is Lilith
who weakens human children when they are small.
That is why I wrote these angels
so that the infant will get well.

    Immediately he took the amulet and
    put it on the infant and it was healed.

# Ssss

The helpers in the Old Aramaic are Swny and Swswny and Snygly; in the Hebrew, Sanvai, Sansanvai, and Semongolof; in the Byzantine, Sisinius, Sines, and Sinodorus; in the Romanian, Sisoe. The constant use of the sibilants and liquids (s, n) is a technique frequently used by singers to warm up— the breath flows uninterrupted through the body and all the muscles begin to relax. The very invocation of the names helps the body control the dread.

## I

*Swny Swswny Snygly*
*in the naming is the breathing,*
*in the saying is the loosening.*
*soony sosoony snygly*

*From iron-sharp Sideros,*
*from the killing of my child.*
*From happenings hard and happenings sharp*
*may I keep far away.*

*like Smamit of old,*
*like women and spiders,*
*lizards and cows—*
*I love my child.*
    *"May the one*
    *who has measured the water*
    *in the hollow of the hand*
*remember us today."*

*Swny Swswny Snygly*
*in the breathing is the naming,*

*Soony Sosoony Snygly*

## II

*Swny Swsyny Sngrw Weartyqw*
*To breathe is to call.*
*To name is to do*
*soony sosoony sangro*

*O Sergius, Sideros, Werzelya*
*deformity, disease, despair*
*kill not my child.*

*Powers of the body,*
*powers of the spirit,*
*powers of the word—*
*I invoke all powers*
*mine and other—*
*KILL NOT MY CHILD!*

*Swny Swswny Sngrw*
*to call is to pray,*
*to say is to sigh.*
*Soony Sosoony Sangro*

## III

*Sanvai, Sansanvai, Semongolof*
*in the breathing is the remembering*
*in the naming is the sound,*
*Sanvai, Sansanvai, Semongolof*

*Hutz Lilith*
*begone the strangler!*
*Away, Ghyllou*
*Far away, the Al*
*Come not near, Karina,*
*Lamaštu, do not approach!*

*Let no evil come near!*
*Let no happening go awry!*
*Let no accident approach!*
*May we live!*

*Sansai Sansanvai Semongolof*
*In the sighing is the power.*
*Sisinious Sines Sinodore*
*in the loosening is the name.*
*Susneyeas, Susneyos*
*Sisoe*
*In the breathing is the hoping,*
*in the saying is the prayer.*

*st zt, I say to you*
*sator*
*saroer*
*s-s-s-s-s-s-s-s-s-s-s-s*

*may we live!*

# The Dread

There is often great poignancy to these incantations and amulets. In them, people name their greatest dread: that something will happen to their child. This dread must be acknowledged, for to suppress it only makes it dig deeper into the soul. Assurances to women that everything will be all right deny the legitimacy of their fears; it is far better to express the fear and anxiety. Incantations, amulets, and other "superstitions" serve this vital function. On the other hand, incantations should not be understood literally. Populating the cosmos with angels and demons can only increase feelings of helplessness and dependence. It is important to realize that the childsnatcher is a projection of dread, not an independent malevolent being who exists "out there" beyond our anxieties. With this caveat, the symbol of the child-snatching demon provides a focus for people's anxieties about pregnancy and birth, and the rituals and incantations are a potent means of acknowledging, expressing, and validating these anxieties. They may also even alleviate the anxieties, for entry into a symbolic universe enables us to make our spiritual and psychological processes visible to ourselves and provides a way for us to enter our own mindbody to create changes there.

It is in this sense that incantations "work." The anthropologist Claude Lévi-Strauss has described the workings of a very long incantation from the Cuna Indians of Panama to facilitate difficult childbirth. In this incantation a shaman comes to a difficult birth at the invitation of the midwife. He must wage combat within the woman's genitals to counter their more evil aspect. The text and shaman provide "a language by means of which unexpressed and otherwise inexpressible psychic states can be immediately expressed." The incantation connects both with the conscious and the unconscious. In the same way, the childsnatcher incantations both tap into the dread of injury and provide cultural assurance that it can be defeated. The value of an incantation against a childsnatcher does not depend on whether or not Michael or Elijah or Solomon ever met a demon and found out her secret names so that she would leave the child alone.

The last few years have brought great advances in our knowledge of the complex interrelationship between mental and physical states. "Imaging" is a recognized therapeutic technique that has measurable influence on biological processes. The impact of this mindbody connection ought to be particularly strong in childbirth, when so much depends on opening, loosening, and untensing the body. Incantations may indeed facilitate childbirth; at the very least, they provide women with a supportive symbolic system for expressing and coping with their fears.

Nevertheless, at first sight it seems unfair to personify this dread as a woman and to pit a male hero against a dangerous female. To make a female the archenemy of human females precisely when they are fulfilling the role that society demands of them seems like the ultimate patriarchal irony. Moreover, Lamashtu and her descendants are classic images of the undomesticated woman: wild eyes; loose, flowing hair; improper dress and toilet. There is a message encoded here: Females who don't conform are dangerous, and females outside the domestic structure may be enemies. The childsnatcher is strong, but she is malevolent. Female is pitted against female, and mothers and would-be mothers are encouraged to enlist the aid of male heroes to keep the demon away. This image of the child-snatching demon-woman seems like a manifestation of the classic fear of woman and of mother that has been so prevalent in Western tradition.

Despite all this, it is important that the childsnatcher be a female figure. Women also have recollections of the Goddess of the Nursery and of the more devouring aspects of their reactions to her. Moreover, they have often internalized this fear to the extent that they not only fear that Mother will devour them but also that they in turn will become devouring mothers themselves. The image of the childsnatcher can enable women to project this fear onto a figure outside themselves and then actively to fight against this figure.

### DREAD

*A screech sounds in the night,*
*and little animals scurry,*
*escaping the owl on the hunt.*

*Mama owl strikes!*
*a little creature is borne away,*
*carried to some far-off nest,*
*where little birds wait.*

*Flight and strike:*
*the awesome power of wings and claws!*
*In an instant,*
*the small running creature is gone.*

*Motherbird feeds the little birdlets,*
*piece by piece*
*dropped softly into their mouths.*
*The power that kills the prey*
*now nourishes.*

*Motherbird hovers*
*protecting her young.*

*Woe to the one who comes to the nest!*
*The protector and the terror are one.*

*Under the wide-spanning wings of Shekhinah*
*we seek our shelter.*
*Suddenly, they flutter,*
*and we are swept away.*

*It is my wing that must shelter you.*
*It is my strength that must protect you.*
*Little as I am to fight the terrors without,*
*I will not be the terror within.*

# Amulets

These prayers and incantations can be written on amulets, physical objects that people may wear on their persons or place in their rooms. Does the amulet bring good fortune? The simple answer, which may be believed by some, is that the amulet has magical properties that will, indeed, bring the desired result. But the real answer is far more complex, for the amulet is a visible prayer—it represents one's hopes and wishes for the desired result, and it may invoke God's help in achieving it. Wearing or looking at such an amulet is a way of offering petitionary prayers.

Amulets that are designed to be worn throughout pregnancy are meant to deter miscarriage. These need not have words on them. They can be specially colored stones reputed to have special properties. One of these may have served as the *eben tekumah* mentioned in the Talmud. A hollow stone, the eagle stone (aetatis) has a long history as a pregnancy amulet.

It contains a second stone within it and was taken as an appropriate symbol for the fetus inside the mother since at least Mesopotamian times. Pictures can also be used on amulets. Both Hellenistic Egyptian uterine amulets and later Jewish tradition use the imagery of the key to the womb. The contemporary Catholic tradition uses a medal with a picture of St. Gerard Majella on one side and Mother and Child on the other.

Amulets take on new significance as labor approaches and the focus shifts from preventing miscarriage to facilitating a safe and healthy delivery. Sometimes the pregnancy amulet could be placed in a different position. The eagle stone, which was worn high throughout pregnancy to help keep the child high within the pregnant woman, was placed lower on her abdomen for delivery. Often, special birthing amulets were made. The ostensible purpose of using amulets is to ensure a speedy delivery. But they have a further nonmagical effect: they bring the mother into the presence of God and align her with the traditional practices of her community of faith.

Birth amulets could be simple stones, like jasper, that were believed to be efficacious. In Egypt, women wore a dwarf made out of clay in honor of the god Bes. In Christian Europe, people brought girdles that were said to have been worn by Mary or by St. Margaret from the churches in which they were kept and laid them on the birthing woman's stomach; in Jewish Europe people used the belts from Torah scrolls or wrapped string around the graves of famous rabbis and then around the birthing woman.

The amulets can have a wide variety of texts. Two silver amulets have been discovered at Ketef Hinnom near Jerusalem which date from the time of the Babylonian Exile in the sixth century B.C.E. These are inscribed with the Priestly Blessing from Numbers 6: 24–26:

*the Lord bless you and protect you,*
*the Lord deal kindly and graciously with you,*
*the Lord bestow favor upon you and grant you well-being*

This amulet may have been generally protective, or it may have been intended for childbirth. Much later, in the twentieth century, Samaritans still hung the priestly blessing on both mother and child:

Angels' names could be inscribed on amulets. *The Testament of Solomon* suggests writing the name Afarof for the angel Raphael. *Sefer HaRazim: the Book of the Mysteries,* an ancient book of Jewish magic from the Greco-Roman period, lists the angels found in a voyage to the heavens. It names the angels found on each step and explains what healings these angels can effect. For the angels of the eighth step we read:

> *If you wish to drive off an evil spirit so that it will not kill her child, before the woman's pregnancy write these angels on a golden lamella and place it in a silver tubular case and let her wear it, and at the time of childbirth take four silver lamellae and write upon them the angels and place them in the four sides of the house and no spirit will come in.*

One could also invoke the great protective deities: Uriel, Raphel, Gabriel, and Michael. With the addition of Nuriel, they form the acronym ARGAMAN, which means "royal purple" in Hebrew. Amulets could also contain Psalm 121 (usually written only with the initial letters of the words), a psalm that was considered particularly appropriate for childbirth and that is translated here on p. 182.

Christian amulets often refer to two events from the Gospels: the births of Jesus and of John the Baptist. Just as Jewish prayers show God's power over birth by evoking God's granting of children to the barren biblical matriarchs, so, too, early

Christian amulets see the birth-giving by the Virgin Mary and the barren Elizabeth as the paradigm of the action of God's Providence in childbirth. The second event is the resurrection of Lazarus. Jesus' saving act in bringing forth the dead Lazarus from the cave is considered the archetype for the action of God in bringing forth the baby to life from the body of its mother. A book of ancient Syriac Christian charms provides:

> For a Woman in Travail:
> Write upon a leaf and give her to swallow:
>> "In the name of the Father and the Son,
>> Lazarus, come forth"
>> (John 11.43)
> or this:
>> "Mary bore Christ,
>> and he silenced all natures."

Medieval prayer-incantations containing these same two motifs could be bound under the mother's right foot, tied on the thigh, or placed on the chest or abdomen. Their purpose is to address the child and tell it to "come forth" and to address the womb: "Be empty, be empty!"

Amulets could also have a long and elaborate text. Throughout Europe it was believed that the story of the life of St. Marguerite could help ensure a speedy delivery. The book containing this story could be placed on a birthing woman's chest or the story could be inscribed on a prayer roll to be placed in an amulet holder and worn around the neck.

The tradition of these amulets began to end after the fifteenth century. The church began to oppose the wearing of amulets and to persecute midwives as witches. The *Malleus Maleficarum* *(Hammer of the Witches)*, which was published in 1486, contains grave warnings against "witch-midwives," and public laws soon followed. As an example, a 1554 English injunction states:

> *A mydwyfe shal not use or exercise any witchcrafte, charmes, sorcerie, invocations or praiers, other than such as be allowable and may stand with the lawes and ordinances of the Catholike Church.*

This attitude, and its accompanying persecution of witches, led ultimately to the elimination of prayers and prayer-amulets during childbirth, and the creation of a silent European birthing scene. The midwives' manuals that have survived from the early-modern period contain no mention of prayers or rituals and are totally "medical" in content. Only remnants escaped the silence, but the life of St. Marguerite (Margaret), told here on pages 128–132, has been found inscribed on small parchment squares as part of a birthing bag (midwife's kit) from Aurillac in Southern France, still in use in the nineteenth century.

# 7. PRAYER

Beyond ritual, amulet, and incantation, there is prayer. In ancient religions, individual gods would often play a role in overseeing childbirth. The Sumerian Nintu, the Greek Artemis, the Egyptian Bes and others, the Roman Lucina all had childbirth as part of their portfolio and were both remembered and implored at each birth. In Judaism and Christianity, people pray directly to God, as in this cycle of Jewish petitions. The monotheist experience of God, however, is ambivalent: at some times people feel that God is intimately involved in their lives and concerned with their affairs; at others, however, God seems remote, eternal, cosmic, beyond the reach of a single human being. People pray for all the many reasons that prayer serves; in addition, when they have petitions, they may seek to magnify their voices by having others, such as friends, family, and clergy, pray for them.

# Birth Patrons

In the same way, people have also invoked lesser spiritual beings. Angels may argue in favor of human beings: an eighteenth-century Jewish prayer compendium, *Seder Baqashos Utehinos*, introduces some of its petitions with a prayer to interceding angels:

*A request for you Michael, Gabriel, Raphael:*

*I pray that you stand before the Holy Blessed One*
*and bring my request*
*that I will be privileged to have pious children.*
*Let my prayer be for you as the sacrifices*
*for we have no temple or sacrifices or high priest . . .*

*I pray also to you, chief-of-staff Metatron:*
*that you should ask the Holy Blessed One*
*that I should bear a Torah scholar . . .*

*You should pray for me before the Holy Blessed One,*
*as you prayed for Elisha the High Priest,*
*that his wife should bear a sage.*
*The Holy Blessed One heard your prayer*
*and she became pregnant and had a son,*
*a Torah sage who was called Rabbi Ishmael the High Priest.*

*So pray for me.*
*And bring me the good news*
*as you brought it to Elisha the High Priest.*

The spirits of the dead may also be viewed as advocates to God. In Judaism, the most powerful intercessor figure is the matriarch Rachel. In the Bible, the prophet Jeremiah has a vision in which he sees Rachel ceaselessly lamenting the exile of her children to Assyria until God relents and assures her that they will return. "Rachel Imenu," Mother Rachel, grows in Jewish legend and ritual to become the chief intercessor before God for the children of Israel, and her tomb in Bethlehem becomes a major site of pilgrimage for Jewish women. Women go there both to pray for conception and to ask for safe delivery. It is perhaps ironic that Rachel, who was barren for so long and who ultimately died in childbirth, should have become the patron of women in these activities, but Jewish women may have felt that she above all women could understand the troubles of women in these matters and could use her privileged position to help other women in difficulty.

In Catholic tradition, the celestial mother who intercedes for her children is Mary, and prayers have been addressed to her in childbirth as also in other moments of distress. Special prayers to Mary as mother may be used, or the standard intercessory prayer, the *Memorare* ("remember"), may be said.

> *Mary,*
> *most pure Virgin and Mother of God,*
> *I remind you of the blessed moment*
> *when for the first time*
> *you saw your newborn Child*
> *and enfolded Him in your arms.*
> *Through this joy of your Motherly Heart,*
> *obtain for me the grace*
> *that I and my child may be protected*
> *from all danger.*

> *Mary,*
> *Mother of my Savior,*
> *I remind you of the unspeakable joy you felt*

*when, after three days of painful seeking,*
*you again found your Divine Son.*
*Through this joy,*
*obtain for me the grace*
*to bring into the world*
*a healthy and well-formed child.*


*Most glorious Virgin Mary,*
*I remind you of the heavenly joy*
*that flooded your Motherly Heart*
*when your Son appeared to you after his Resurrection.*
*Through this great joy*
*obtain for my child*
*the blessings of Holy Baptism*
*so that my child may be admitted to the Church,*
*the Mystical Body of your Divine Son.*


# St. Marguerite

In the Middle Ages, a virgin martyr, St. Marguerite (Margaret), was a most popular patron of childbirth. Women prayed at her altars and shrines, and touching her reliquary or even a book of her life was believed to be efficacious in childbirth. Despite the fact that the Church condemned such beliefs, they were not abandoned, and a number of early-modern French prayers to St. Marguerite have survived.

St. Marguerite is reputed to have lived in the third or fourth century in Antioch. She is first mentioned in the West in the ninth century and becomes one of the most beloved saints of the late Middle Ages. The legend of her life relates how she was exiled from her father's house for converting to

Christianity, how she resisted the advances of a pagan cult official, and suffered torture and ultimately death. In prison, she had a miraculous encounter with the devil: in the form of a dragon, it devoured her—but she emerged from its belly unharmed. When she was about to be executed, she prayed to God that God would grant mercy to "those who remember me and call upon me in their distress and women who invoke me in birth." Latin manuscripts of her life exist from as early as the tenth century. A devotional treatise in French, *La vie de madame saincte marguerite,* was composed in the twelfth century and widely copied. Rabelais mentions how it was read to women in labor; a verse in *Miroir de nostre Dame* reports how it would be placed on their breasts, and some copies were clearly made as amulets.

The French prayers to Marguerite relate her story and invoke her help. The following prayer comes from the fifteenth century:

### A MADAME SAINCTE MARGUERITE
### ORAISON LIMINAIRE

*Madame St. Margaret,*
*honored virgin of God most high*
*who for the love of God our Lord*
*suffered torments and martyrdom;*
*who made many requests of God*
*when they were about to cut off your head,*
*and especially that a woman*
*large with child, who turns to you, O Lady*
*with heart devout*
*and asks for your aid:*
*that God keep her from dying*
*and tarry not to help her.*

*I pray you, honored virgin,*
*noble and fortunate martyr,*
*that you pray to God for me*
*and sweetly supplicate him.*
*So that in his compassion he will comfort me*
*and open well the load that I carry.*
*Without danger to spirit or body,*
*make this load issue forth!*
*That I, rejoicing, may see it with many glances*
*and that I may, all of my life,*
*thank you for your great beneficence.*
    *So let it be!*

During the Protestant Reformation, Martin Luther ob-
jected to reading these "St. Margaret legends and Old Wives'
tales." In Catholic southern France, prayers to Marguerite continued to be recited until quite recently. The following such
prayer was found in a book printed in 1770: This prayer, in
more modern French, beseeches that the child be born at the
right time, and that it be baptized as soon as it be born.

### PRAYER TO INVOKE ST. MARGARET
### WHEN A WOMAN IS IN LABOR

*Illustrious St. Marguerite,*
*whose virtues and merit*
*have procured for you in heaven*
*a most glorious throne:*

*Who from your tenderest infancy,*
*consecrated your innocence*
*to the Spouse of chastity,*
*the God of all purity.*

*Who in the course of your life,*
*filled with a thousand miracles,*
*by trampling the furious dragon,*
*knew how to put out its rage.*

*Who suffered with courage,*
*the supplications and anger*
*of your cruel prosecutors.*

*Who, as the prize of your victory,*
*rule at the Seat of Glory,*
*tasting the delights of heaven*
*with the fortunate spirits.*

*I implore, triumphant virgin,*
*your powerful protection,*
*your merits and your credit*
*before the savior Jesus Christ.*

*This divine savior agrees,*
*in his great compassion,*
*to everything that you ask*
*for mortals in misfortune.*

*Behold the state in which I sigh!*

*Obtain for me, virgin martyr,*
*that the Lord, by His favors,*
*will help me in my pains.*
*May He save and comfort me*
*and the fruit that my body carries,*
*that it may be born on the destined day,*
*and that as soon as it is born*
*—thanks to his supreme goodness—*

*it may receive holy baptism,*
*so that it may live in sanctity*
*in time and eternity.*

In the last several hundred years, devotion has grown for St. Gerard Majella, as patron of childbirth. Women carry the motherhood prayer and wear a St. Gerard medal; Catholic hospitals often have statues and pictures of St. Gerard in the maternity ward. A holy card contains this prayer for intercession in behalf of a safe delivery:

*. . . thou hast been raised up by God*
*as the Patron and Protector of expectant mothers.*
*Preserve me from danger and from the excessive pains*
*    accompanying childbirth,*
*and shield the child that I now carry,*
*that it may see the light of day and receive the lustral waters of*
*    baptism . . .*

# A Cycle of Mystical Jewish Prayers

The European Jewish tradition has prayers that are meant to be said by the pregnant woman and/or her husband. Among these are several that have been preserved in a number of different forms. They are found in Hebrew in little prayer books that were written by hand in the eighteenth century for Italian Jewish women and in the *Kitsur Shelah*, a seventeenth-century Eastern European compendium of Jewish teachings intended for men. The same prayers are also found in Old Yiddish and Yiddish, in printed prayer books and instruction manuals written for women from the eighteenth century on.

The four prayers that follow are full of allusions to Jewish mysticism and folklore. They form a learned literary tradition that was carried throughout the European Jewish world and translated into its languages.

These prayers are not in our idiom. The metaphors and symbols, the cadences and emotions, do not come readily to our lips. And yet, there is a special magic in studying the prayers that women said several hundred years ago.

## ON READING ANCIENT PRAYERS

*I sit and enter an ancient world.*
*I look at the voices of long ago.*
*Unfamiliar thoughts surround me:*
    *clouds of judgment,*
    *holes in the divine throne,*
    *prosecutors from the Other Side,*
        *God plugs the entry way,*
        *fiery angels*
        *collect the cries of laboring women.*
*Righteous advocates plead for compassion,*
*Deers stretch their horns toward God.*
*Strange symbols from another world.*

*Through the mists of antique midrash,*
*phrases arise to greet me:*
    *A proper seed . . .*
    *an auspicious time . . .*
    *a living child . . .*
    *The key of Birth . . .*
    *to open the womb.*
    *Have compassion . . .*
    *Answer me . . .*

*Let no injury come!*
  *let me not labor in vain!*
*I see before me eons of pregnant women*
    *praying in the languages of the world.*
*I feel their hopes and fears,*
    *for they are mine.*
*The years dissolve,*
*strange symbols become familiar,*
*I join my voice to theirs.*

*O God, as You have had compassion*
    *on eons of good women,*
    *have compassion on me.*
*May I too give birth quickly,*
    *as a chicken lays an egg,*
*to a living seed of Holiness*
    *who will grow to serve You.*

*May our past reach into the future,*
*Amen.*

# Like a Hen

The first of these prayers is on behalf of a pregnant woman. In some Yiddish traditions, the woman says it for herself at labor. In the Italian tradition, the woman says "Like a Hen" and the *"zera qayyama"* together (in Hebrew) every day from the beginning of the seventh month on. But the prayer could also be used as an intercessory prayer for someone else to pray for the well-being of the pregnant woman. In the *Kitsur Shelah*, a seventeenth-century book of Jewish teachings from Eastern Europe, the husband is instructed to say it daily from the time his wife enters the seventh month. An early Yiddish compendium, the *Seder Baqashos Utehinos*, preserves it in two forms: in Hebrew as a prayer that a sage or Rabbinical students should say in behalf of the woman from the seventh month on, and in Yiddish as an intercessory prayer for a woman to say for her daughter or her sister. It thus offers women family members an opportunity and language to pray for one another.

"Like a Hen" begins with an invocation to God to lighten the trouble of pregnancy and to exempt the woman from the judgment of Eve that women would give birth in pain, so that she will give birth easily as a hen lays an egg, and that the child be born in an auspicious hour for all good fortune:

*May it be your will, O God and the God of my ancestors,*
*that you should ease the trouble of pregnancy for* _____
*and you should give her strength all the days of her pregnancy*
*that neither her strength nor the strength of her fetus should weaken*
    *in any respect.*
*Rescue her from the writ of Eve!*

*And when it is time for her to give birth,*
*may her contractions not overpower her,*
*and let the birthling come out to the air of the world*
    *in an instant*
*and let her give birth easily as a hen lays an egg*
*with no damage to her or to the birthling.*

*May it be born at a good hour and a good sign*
*for life and peace and health,*
*for grace and lovingkindness,*
*and wealth and honor.*

The Hebrew and the Yiddish versions of this prayer continue with a petition for the health and well-being of the woman and her child. Several Hebrew versions of the prayer make a strange request: that the woman not go into labor on the Sabbath. Jewish law is very clear—everything that can be done for a woman in labor should be done. There can be no hesitation that something might be in violation of the Sabbath, because the Sabbath *must* be violated for the woman and her child. Nevertheless, the Sabbath is being violated, and it is a mark of the particular piety of this prayer that people pray that this not be necessary. In the same fashion, in another prayer a woman prays that she not desire anything unkosher during her pregnancy. If she desires it, it would be given to her, because of the belief that a pregnant woman's cravings arise from the needs of the fetus. So the pious woman prays that such cravings never arise.

> *And may she not give birth on the Sabbath*
> *so that, God forbid,*
> > *people do not have to violate the Sabbath for her.*

> *And may all my requests*
> > *be fulfilled in good measure*
> > *with saving compassion*
> *in the midst of Israel who are in need of compassion.*

> *Do not send me away empty from before You. Amen.*

# Zera Qayyama:
## "A Proper Living Seed"

In the tradition of the Italian prayer books, "Like a Hen" is combined with another prayer, *"Zera Qayyama"* ("A Proper Living Seed"). The pregnant woman recites both from the seventh month on. She is to fast and give charity to the poor according to her ability. Then, every day until she gives birth, she recites these prayers as part of the fixed daily prayers, at the end of the eighteen benedictions (the Amidah) before "the one who makes peace." In the Yiddish book of prayers, *Seder Baqashos Utehinos*, "A Proper Living Seed" is a separate prayer, to be recited from the seventh month on, evenings and mornings during the Amidah, on weekdays at the petitionary prayer "Don't Send Us Away from You Empty-handed," and on Sabbath (when the six petitionary prayers are not said) at the end before "the One who Makes Peace." This prayer is then cited in Hebrew, even though the rest of the book is Yiddish prayers. These notations indicate that, contrary to what our knowledge of later European Jewish gender roles would indicate, in the seventeenth and eighteenth centuries both the Yiddish- and Italian-speaking communities expected women to recite the full daily prayers in Hebrew.

The *Kitsur Shelah* accompanies this prayer with a striking ritual. When the woman enters her ninth month of pregnancy, the husband and wife should fast. In the evening before they eat they should give charity to proper poor people and settle their affairs. Then they should each face the wall in opposite directions, recite two *Anenu* litanies, and say this prayer.

The prayer begins with a request for compassion and a reminder to God that God alone is the one who holds the key of birthing. Therefore, the supplicant asks God that she may give birth expansively to a proper living seed from the Holy

Side. Even though the prayers are all in Hebrew, this phrase is given in Aramaic: *zera' qayyama wekasher mesitra dequdsha*. The phrase evokes the world of Jewish mysticism, which seeks to help defend Holiness from The Other Side, the demonic World. The prayer continues with reference to David's supplicatory psalms and asks that her prayers be granted as were David's, and then it ends with an invocation of God's help to the foremothers.

> O God and God of my ancestors:
> Have mercy on all the birthing women of Israel
>      and among them your handmaid _____.
> I cast my supplication before You,
>      O merciful and gracious One,
>      merciful are Your mercies
>
> And in Your hand is the key of birthing
>      which has not been placed in the hands of an agent.
>
> Therefore, remember Your compassion and Your grace,
>      O Lord our God who desires life.
> Take note of me in mercy
> And let me give birth expansively
> to proper living seed from the Holy Side.
>
> And bring to fulfillment in me
> that which was said by King David, may he rest in peace,
>      "In straights I called upon You,
>      You answered me in expansiveness.
>      The Lord is with me, I shall not fear."
>
> May the One who heard the prayer of the King of Israel
>      hear my prayer.
> And by the merit of my forefathers and my foremothers,

*May the one who answered our holy mothers*
       *Sarah, Rivka, Rachel, Leah and Hannah*
       *and all the righteous proper and pious women*
*answer me.*

# The Judgment Prayer

The prayer begins with an acknowledgment that the judgment on Eve was proper but reminds God that God has total discretion in these matters: "Who will say to you, 'What are you doing?'" It therefore requests that God allow an easy birth to the woman, by the merit of all the righteous people who have gone before and whom God allowed an easy birth.

The prayer then brings us into a world of judgment, of spirits who speak on behalf of humanity and those who speak against it, and of God who sits on the throne and decides the fate of humans. A famous mishnah stresses the importance of the three special commandments for women (consecrating a portion of bread dough to God, observing the menstrual regulations, and lighting the Sabbath candles) by declaring that for failing to observe them, women may die in childbirth. The Talmud explains that childbirth is a time of danger when a woman is tested for righteousness; men are tested while crossing bridges and at other similar moments of danger. This judgment is held in the heavenly court, with prosecuting and defending attorneys.

This prayer also builds on a scene in the Midrash *Pesikta deRav Kahana* in which the angels wish to prevent the wicked King Menashe's prayers from reaching God, so they block up the windows of heaven. But God digs a hole underneath his throne so that Menashe's prayers can rise up to him. Our prayer now begs God to stop up these holes so that the prose-cutor's voice cannot rise to heaven.

> O Lord of Hosts who sits among the cherubs,
>> who judges righteously with truth:
> You have rebuked and punished us
>> since the creation of humanity,
> that we women should give birth with sorrow.
> As it is written,
>> "In pain you will birth your children."

> But—everything is at Your discretion,
> everything is in Your hand:
> the one on whom You have mercy is mercied,
>> the one on whom You have compassion has found compassion.
> Nobody can change what You do,
> And who can say to You, "What are You doing?"

> O God, have compassion on me
>> for the sake of Your great compassion
> And for the merit of the righteous ones
> and by the merit of all the righteous women
>> upon whom You have had compassion.
> You listened and paid heed to their cries
>> when they called out to You,
> You opened their wombs in lovingkindness and compassion
> and they gave birth in lovingkindness.
> The hinges of their wombs opened
>> at the appropriate time.

> O Lord my God,
> You existed before the creation of the world,
>> and You bear the world for all eternity,
>> with Your great lovingkindness.

*Take away my guilt,*
*Don't enter judgment with me, Your servant.*
*Do not listen to the voice of the angels*
    *who prosecute me before You.*
*Block up every gap in Your holy throne*
*so that their cries will not come up before You.*
*Allow no place for my prosecution*
    *to rise before Your throne of glory.*


*And the righteous angels,*
    *The truthful advocates,*
*the ones who teach and speak*
    *and advocate defense and merit*
*For Your whole people and for me;*
*To them incline Your ear and listen*
    *and accept their word and their defense,*
    *and answer their intercession,*
    *and answer their petition immediately,*
    *and let them stand always before You,*
        *to be our advocates of truth, righteousness and merit.*


The woman then asks God to take the key so that the child be born easily, to make the child good and protect it, and to accept her prayers as God accepted Hannah's:

*Take the key of pregnancy in Your right hand*
    *and open my pregnancy*
*without pain or sorrow or damage or fault.*


*And weaken the evil impulse in the boy or girl*
    *that comes from my loins*
*and strengthen the good impulse in it.*

And protect me and the birthling
    whatever it may be—boy or girl
from all evil spirits and evil ghosts
And may the evil eye have no power over us.


O Lord, God of hosts
Listen and hear the sound of my entreaty
and place my tears in Your jug and in Your
    treasury.
and accept them
    as You accepted the prayer and tears of
        Hannah
    sending Your holy spirit
      on Eli the Priest,
    sending glad tidings to her through him.
For thus he said to her:
    "Go in peace,
    and the Lord God of Israel
    will grant the request you asked of him"    (I Sam. 1:17)
For in Your mercy,
    You are prepared,
    to accept the prayers
    of those who turn to You in truth.


May the words of my mouth
    and the meditation of my heart
    be acceptable to You,
    O Lord, my rock and my redeemer.

# The Doe and the Fiery Creatures

Like the other prayers in this ancient cycle, this prayer includes the key, the prosecutor, and the seed. It also adds a wish for a good child, for milk to feed the child and strength to raise it. The prayer exists in both Yiddish and Hebrew, with instructions in Yiddish to begin to recite it in the seventh month and in Italian, at birth. The Hebrew version, found in Bela Yudita's Italian prayer book, contains long sentences that are in Aramaic. This may be an indication that the original prayer, and possibly the entire cycle, was originally composed in this language.

The deer section interweaves two separate biblical passages. In Psalm 42:2, we read, "As a deer yearns for water courses, my soul yearns for You, O God." Job 39:1–3 talks about the does giving birth: "Do you know the time of birth of the wild goats and watch over the labor of does? Do you count the months as they are completed so that you know when it is time for them to give birth? Then they bow down and fear for their children and send forth their labor pains."

The fiery creatures bring us back to the courtroom scene. In Bela Yudita's prayer book they are called *yetedot*, literally "tent pegs." In the Yiddish version they are called *yetsirot*, "creatures."

*Please, O Lord of Hosts:*
*Look upon the suffering of Your servant*
    *and remember and do not forget Your servant,*
    *and give Your servant human seed.*

*May the God of Israel grant me my petition*
*Your servant implores you*
    *as a doe yearns at the water courses*

*at the time that she seeks to give birth.*
*and her pains grow hard upon her.*
She yearns for You with her horns
and bitterly cries for Your mercy.

For the key of birthing is in Your hand.
You pity her and open her womb
in compassion and lovingkindness.

Just so my soul yearns for You, O God,
and asks for Your mercy and lovingkindness
to open the hinges of my womb
so that I may give birth
to the birthling within me
in an hour appropriate for birth
at a time of blessing and salvation.
With a living child,
so that I do not struggle for naught,
labor in vain, God forbid.
In Your hand alone is the key of birthing
as it is written
"And God remembered Rachel
and listened to her
and opened her womb."

May you be moved by my petition
as from the depths of my heart
I call upon the Lord.
My voice calls to You:
answer me from Your holy mountain. Selah.
Listen to my prayer,
and may the entreaty
that I call before You in full heart
come before You in friendship and happiness.

*The angels above*
*who are appointed over the birth stool*
*who are noble fire*
*and called* yesirot *[creatures]*

[May the spirits appointed over the birth
    stool
    who are called in heaven *yetedot*(!)
take the voices of women
and place them before that palace
when the Other Side comes to prosecute.

At that hour,
    which is an hour of danger—
they arise and lift their voices
    before the one who is appointed over
    the door
and the Other Side cannot prosecute.]

*My prayer comes to You:*
*You commanded us to be fruitful and multiply*
*and to raise children for Torah and Mitzvot*
    *to stand before You,*
    *serve You and bless Your name.*

*Do not allow space for the Other Side*
    *to accuse me or the fruit in my belly.*
*Remember me for good,*
    *Do not forget Your servant*
*Give your servant a holy living seed.*

*The Lord of Hosts is with us,*
    *the God of Jacob is our fortress, Selah.*          (Ps. 46:12)

*O Lord of Hosts,*
*blessed be the person who trusts in You.*                    (Ps. 84:13)
*The Lord redeems, the King answers us on the day*
*    we call.*                                                 (Ps. 19:15)

# A Month of Anticipation
## The Counting-up Ritual

When the ninth month comes, celebration, anticipation, and impatience grow. It is time for ritual. The Counting-up Ritual focuses on the coming child and the community it comes into, counting up to the day of the child's coming rather than down to the end of the pregnancy. Both Judaism and Christianity have seasons of anticipation that are marked by a daily counting of the days that pass. The counting is often accompanied by the use of calendars that mark the days. In Judaism, one "counts the Omer," to span the period between the spring festival of Passover that celebrates freedom from slavery and the early-summer festival of Shavuot that celebrates the revelation at Sinai. In Christianity, the counting season is Advent, the days that lead up to Christmas. The counting during these periods is important; it builds anticipation and prepares the one who counts for the event to come, which in both cases is the revelation and formation of something new. Like the Omer and Advent, the ninth month of pregnancy looks forward to a new universe.

This ritual focuses on the family and friends of the pregnant woman. It creates a bond of care and reminds the woman that she is not alone and that she is part of a cosmic picture. The ritual is performed by the woman, either in solitude or in the company of her children and/or her partner.

## THE COUNTING-UP RITUAL

ON THE FIRST DAY OF THE NINTH MONTH:

The pregnant woman and her partner, family and/or friends make a counting calendar. One can mark each day on the calendar with the name of a person, living or dead, who is meaningful to the pregnant woman. These names constitute the spiritual community that the child is joining. If the woman is so inclined, she may want to gather photographs to place on the calendar. It is good to have forty people, for the ninth month is sometimes preternaturally long. Each woman/family should decide the order of the names and make some provision to honor those whose days come after the birth.

EVERY DAY BEFORE THE BIRTH:

1. *Start the ritual formally.*

   A ritual is started by marking off the sacred time and space. One should perform a bodily action connected with ritual acts: e.g., bowing, making the sign of the cross, taking three steps forward and back, making the sign of a circle. Then one could light a large candle which will be lit and snuffed out each day of this month.

2. *Count the day.*

   Recite the passage of time: "Today is the thirteenth day of the ninth month of my pregnancy."

3. *Name the person.*

   Using the advent calendar, name aloud the person for the day. Remember that person with thoughts, prayers, and blessings. If the person is alive, resolve to write or phone him or her this day, and do so. If the person is no longer living, recite and, if possible, record a memory of that person to share with the child much later.

4. *Give charity.*

The child is coming not only to this community, but to the world. Our larger community of care is the whole world, and in the ninth month women should give donations for the care of the world. One donation should be for social justice, poverty relief, and education. How much is a matter of means. Do you have enough money to twin your child by sponsoring a foster child? Do you have enough money to put several coins in a box or jar every day and let the money accumulate into one donation? According to our means, we need to care for all humanity.

We also need to care for the earth, and one donation should be for our environment. Do you have enough money to plant a tree every day so that there will be a grove growing in honor of your child? Do you want to put a little aside to save the rainforest or fight air pollution? With these donations we remember the special person of each day in whose honor we make the donation, and we remember that we and the child come to the world with a sacred trust to care for it and for one another.

5. *a meditation*

> *In the image of God I am created.*
> *In the image of God you are formed.*
> *In the image of God we all are made.*

> *We are the stewards of the world,*
> *formed "to work and preserve her."*     (Gen. 2:15)
> *Ours is to keep creation whole,*

*preserve the world alive.*
*Much is the labor, arduous the task,*
*but no one person must complete it.*

*Into the chain of being we come,*
*people of the once, the now and the future,*
*people I love, people I do not know.*

*You come into a world of love*
*and a world of trouble and challenge.*
*We are here to receive your gifts*
*and bestow ours upon you.*

*In this world, I reach to others*
*and seek to reach beyond myself.*
*We are mated in the tasks of the world,*
*partners in the acts of creation.*

*We welcome you with shared blessing.*
*Welcome to the sacred task,*
*to the dance of a life with love,*
*the song of a life in joy.*

6. *End the ritual.*

For closure, count the day again, snuff out the candle, and
perform the same body act with which you began.

# Thoughts for the Ninth Month

Sometimes the time seems very long.

God, if you are also a woman,
    why does it take nine months for me to give
        birth?
Why, if you are also a woman,
could you not have thought to make me like you?
    For you created the world in a day,
        created the universe in six days
    and then had earned your rest.


God, if you are also a woman,
surely you should have understood:
    I too would like to create in a day,
    to give birth in a week, in a month,
    to rest with my daughter, my son.


God, since you are also a woman,
    why must I be pregnant forever?


But a child is not a universe,
    speaking is not birth,
    creating is not loving.
I, too, gave birth—
    to my beloved Ephraim,
    my first-born, Israel,
And this birth was not short,
was not easy,
had no rest.

I started at Sinai, at the mountain of Pentecost,
    mating my laws to the unformed people—
    a conception, a beginning.
The month of Sivan,                            (Exod. 19:1)
the third month of the year.

I saw them kicking, squirming, complaining—
    a rocky gestation,
    full of false starts
    and almost-endings.

I waited for the growth of my child,
    waited till I would have my people,
    waited till it seemed like forever.

My wait was longer than yours:
    forty-one years
    till the people were born onto their land.
toward Passover,
    the month of Nisan,                    (Josh. 4:19)
    the first month of the year.
Forty-one years
and nine months.

And as you wait your nine months,
Remember the birth of Israel,
remember me.

Pregnancy is long, I say.
Birth is not easy.
Children are not easy.

# 8. Awaiting the Hour

As labor nears, it is time to make the birth area a sacred place for the process of birth and to enter the holy time of the birthing ritual. The atmosphere surrounding the labor and birth conveys powerful messages to the birthing woman, influences the birth itself, and leaves a lasting impression on the mother. In the typical modern hospital, birth is treated as a medical event in which scientific medicine brings a baby into the world. Hospital gowns, enemas, monitors, cervical checks all convey the message that it is only when technology conquers nature that children can be born.

Birth in homes and in birthing suites is more personal, often family oriented, and respectful of natural processes. Nevertheless, sometimes we get absorbed in the mechanics of birthing and concentrate on the body processes alone. At the moment of birth it doesn't matter, for the majesty and the sacredness of the moment fill whatever space it is in. But the hours of labor often can be enriched when the space and the woman are surrounded by holiness, and a sacred atmosphere can enable a woman to integrate the spiritual experience of birth with her other experiences of divinity.

# Wall Amulets

Wall amulets have traditionally been concerned with the protection of the child and mother against the child-snatching demon. They are designed to be hung on the wall of the birthing room, and they frequently bear the statement "Adam and Eve, begone Lilith" and the names Sanvai, Sanvanai, and Semongolof, the three angels who fight against Lilith. Many copies have been made of an amulet that first appears in the 1701 printed edition of the amulet maker's handbook, *Sefer Raziel*, which was first written in the eleventh century.

At the top are the names of angels. Inside the borders are, on the right, the seals of Sanvai, Sansanvai, and Semongolof as they also appear in earlier manuscripts of *Sefer Raziel* and above them the words "Adam and Eve, begone Lilith." On the left are the same words over birdlike pictures of Sanvai, Sansanvai, and Semongolof with their names inscribed. Underneath is a formal adjuration:

*I adjure you, first Eve,*
*by the name of the one who created you*
*And by the names of the three angels*
*that your creator sent after you*
*and the angel in the sea islands.*

*You swore to them*
*that wherever their names would be found*
*you will not injure*
*Not you, and not any of your servants and attendants,*
*not anyone who will carry their names.*

*Therefore by their names*
*and their seals that are written here,*
*I adjure you and your servants and attendants*
*that you should not hurt the birthing mother*
*and not the child that is born to her.*
*Not by day and not by night*
*not through their food nor through their drink.*
*Not in their head and not in their heart*
*and not in their 248 limbs and 365 sinews.*

*By the power of these names and seals,*
*I adjure you and your servants and attendants.*

*Sefer Raziel* also contains another major childbirth amulet. On the outside of the design are the names of the four rivers of Paradise. This puts us at the primordial beginning, in the heart of the garden of Eden. The design has two circles, and between them is inscribed: "**Adam and Eve, begone Lilith the first Eve. Shamriel, Hasdiel, Sanvai, Sansanvai, Semongolof.**" Then comes **KWZW BMWKSZ KWZW**, the fourteen-letter name of God, created by writing the Hebrew words "YHWH ELHYNW YHWH, "YHWH (The Lord) Our God the Lord"

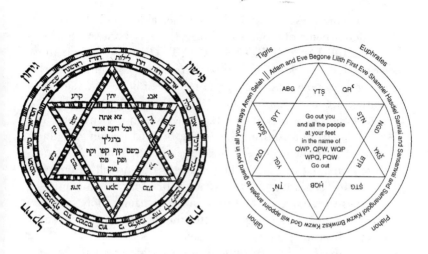

and substituting the letter that comes after it in the alphabet for each letter of this phrase. The circle then continues with a phrase from Psalm 91:11, "**For God will appoint for you angels to guard you in all your ways**," written with the initial letters of each verse. "**Amen. Selah.**"

Inside the second circle are two triangles arranged in a hexagram. Within this hexagram are the words "**Go out, you and all the people at your feet**," a verse with important connotations for childbirth (explained on pp. 221–222) and then a special charm: "**In the name of qwp, qpw, wqp, wpq pqw.**" These three letters are the initials of *qedusha we purqana* "holiness and deliverance." They are especially appropriate because in the permutation "**PWQ**," they spell the Aramaic command "Go out!" The later version of the same amulet places the two triangles on top of each other so that the top word is "**Go out**" in Hebrew and the bottom word is "**Go out**" in Aramaic.

Around these two triangles is a special formula, the forty-two-letter name of God: ABG, YTṢ QRʿ ŚṬN NGD YKŠ BṬR ṢTG ḤQB ṬNʿ **YGL PZQ ŠQW ṢYT**. The triads include the words "Destroy Satan" but probably represent the initial letters of some formula. Rashi, the great teacher of Bible and Talmud, writing a commentary about 1100 C.E. on the Talmudic passage, knows of a forty-two-letter name (which is mentioned in the Talmud) but does not know the original meaning of the formula. There is a prayer, *"Anna Bekoach,"* the initial letters of which spell out this name. This prayer is traditionally ascribed to the first-century mystic R. Nehunya ben Hakana and understood as the source of the forty-two-letter name. More probably, the prayer was composed after the date of Rashi and was created from the letters of the name.

All these childbirth amulets are magical, but at the same time they are profoundly religious. They recall the great saving deeds of God and the might and concern that God has shown human beings, and they pray for God's help in the birthing. They are visual, graphic, and tangible prayers, and they bring sanctity to the space in which they are hung.

# The Sacred Circle

The room has been graced with a prayerful reminder of God's presence, and it is time to magnify the sanctity of the birthing bed or chair. It is time to define the area of the *temenos,* the sacred zone. We can draw the boundaries on the floor, or mark them with strings and ribbons, or establish them by the presence of people. By so doing, we create a sacred circle. The round belly of the woman has itself been the sacred circle that protected the child and contained the power of creation. Now that special space must be enlarged:

*In the magic circle, you are safe.*
*I was your magic circle:*
*I willed, protected, and surrounded you.*
*I kept you from the world,*
        *from its accidents and demons,*
        *its bacteria and muses,*
        *its viruses and hatred and violence and envy.*
*In the circle of my being,*
*you were safe.*

*I have stretched very large—*
*but still I am too small for you.*
*The circle that once protected you now constricts.*
*The safe space in which you grew ready*
*no longer lets you move.*

*Now you must come out.*

*Behold, I create a new space,*
*a circle drawn around us both.*
*The circle of me gives way to the circle of we.*

*I draw this circle:*
        *with flour strewn on the floor,*
        *with ribbons and strings and bows,*
        *with people gathering around.*

*The space must be sacred,*
*the hour is holy.*
*The coming is now.*
*To our presence*
*and the presence of the Presence,*
*blessed be the one who comes in the name of the Lord.*

## WALK AROUND ZION

——— ✲ ———

The space should also be consecrated by being walked. The woman herself might walk around it and then sit in the center. Her friends and attendants then surround her:

> Sobu Tsiyyon wehaqifuha
> sipru migdaleha
> *Walk around Zion,*
> *surround her, note her towers.* (Ps. 48:3)

*Circumambulation!*
*Surround*
*and mark!*

*From the circle of this body*
*to the circle of this birth,*
*around and around.*

*Circle the walls of Jericho,*
*mark and make a noise.*
*Shout for the presence of God.*
*Walls will give way.*

*Walk the walls of Jerusalem,*
*surround the walls of Woman*
*Call the Presence of God*
*to come forth,*
*to bring forth,*
*to be.*

# A Modern Wall Plaque

Wall amulets are visible reminders of the presence of God. When a woman looks at such a plaque during labor, she is continually reminded of the support of her tradition and of the presence of God. Modern methods of birth also call for the use of an object or plaque as a focal point, a devise to aid concentration and relaxation. If the focal point has personal significance, it creates a sense of continuity with the rest of the woman's life. If the focal point is a religious amulet, the moment is infused with a sense of divine presence and of spiritual awareness.

But what amulet? Antiquarians might enjoy using ancient Christian or Jewish examples, but most people would not find them aesthetically or spiritually uplifting. It may be more meaningful to design new wall plaques, based on the traditions of the old, but conforming to modern sensibilities. I designed the wall plaque presented here together with a calligrapher, Betsy Plotkin Teutsch. It is designed as a work of art that a family can treasure as a sign and remembrance of the birth, much as Jews commission and treasure ceremonial marriage contracts (ketubot). People who are interested can use this design, or can work to develop one of their own.

In this amulet-plaque, the upper left and lower right corners continue the traditions of the anti-childsnatcher plaques.

May יהוה answer you in the time of your trouble answer you. "...." May the One who answers the pregnant woman during labor answer you.

Raise up your heads O Gates, raise yourselves, you everlasting doors, and let the King of Glory come. This is the Gate for God; let the righteous enter

God brought me out to a broad space and delivered me.

May the One who answers the mother in the time of her troubles answer you.

In straits I called upon Yah, and God answered me expansively

The upper left spells out *Adam VeHava Hutz Lilit.* "Adam and Eve, begone Lilith!" but with the words arranged in a new way to spell out *El,* "God." The lower right has the pictures and names of the three protective angels Sanvai, Sansanvai, and Semongalof as they appear in the famous 1701 amulet illustrated on p. 153.

Also around the margins are two more icons, an old image, the key of birthing, and a new image, the waiting hands of the birth attendant preparing to welcome the child.

These icons frame the central design, which is intended to evoke at one and the same time the womb riding the waves of contractions, the cosmic egg floating on the oceanic waters, and the cervix opening between the knees of the laboring woman.

The words out of which this wall plaque is constructed are verses from the Psalms and from rabbinic writings, verses that are very meaningful in the context of childbirth and are used in the poems and prayers for labor and delivery that follow.

The words within the central oval emphasize the role of the vagina as the sacred gateway to life. They come from verses said at the entrance to the holy Temple. At the top and bottom are the words of the child "Open for me the righteous gates, let me come through them and praise Yah," taken from Psalm 118:19. The gates that are opening within are themselves made from verses from the Psalms. The right gate reads, at the top, "This is the gate for God" (Ps. 118:20). Beneath it

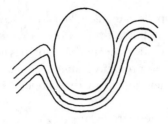

are the verses from Psalm 24:3–6, **Who may rise in God's holy place? The one who is clean of hands and pure of heart, who has not taken a false mortal oath, never sworn deceitfully. That one will receive blessing from the Lord, reward from God our deliverer. This is the generation of those who seek God, who desire your presence, Jacob, Selah.**
The left gate continues with Psalm 24:7:

**Raise up your heads, O gates, raise yourselves, you everlasting doors, and let the king of glory come.**

The waves/thighs surrounding the oval also begin with verses from the Psalms which refer to God's saving presence in times of distress, and they are eerily appropriate to birth. On the right is the opening verse of Psalm 121, a traditional psalm for reading during labor, **"I lift my eyes to the hills; from where does my help come?"** On the left is a verse from Psalm 118:3, also sometimes used in birthing prayers, **"In straits I called upon Yah, and God answered me expansively."** In the second row is Psalm 118:26, **"Blessed be the one who comes in the name of the Lord."** The first line that goes under the oval quotes Psalms 118:7, 17, and 20 **"When I was in straits I called upon Yah . . . God saved me from the cosmic waters, . . . and brought me out to a broad space. God delivered me for God delights in me."**

The bottom two waves contain two Aramaic quotes from Rabbinic midrash which seem to preserve ancient formulas.

Both are preserved in the *Midrash Tehilim*, a midrashic commentary on the book of Psalms. The section on Psalm 20, a traditional birthing psalm, contains this comment on verse 2:

> *"The Lord will answer you in the day of distress."* Rabbi Joshua Hakohen says, "There are nine verses in this Psalm, corresponding to the nine months that a woman is pregnant with a child. And what do they say? "May the One who answers the pregnant woman during labor answer you."

The midrash also records a tradition of saying a comforting formula to the pregnant woman:

> Said R. Shimon B. Lakish, "A pregnant woman is having difficulty giving birth, and they say to her, 'We don't know what to say to you, but the One who answered your mother at the time of her troubles will answer you at the time of your troubles' "

When these verses, which can and should be recited during labor, are written on a focal-point plaque and placed in the birthing room, they grace and sacralize the birthing space.

# The Sacred Moment: Preparing the Woman

## UNBINDING

—— ∞ ——

The sacred space is ready; it is time to mark the sacredness of the hour, the ritual time of labor and birth. The laboring woman is the celebrant of this ritual, and she is the one to mark its beginning. The first step is to move out of ordinary time, to leave mundane time by removing from herself the articles of her regular clothing. Moreover, it has been traditional in many societies to undo all fastenings and bonds, including removing all hair pins. The symbolism of this act is clear: it undoes any obstructions and hindrances that could get in the way of a clear and smooth delivery. The Romans made the symbolism explicit in a birth prayer that women in labor offered to the goddess Lucina:

> Say ye,
> "Thou, Lucina, has bestowed on us the light of life."
> Say ye,
> "You hear the prayer of women in travail.
> But let her who is with child
>     unbind her hair before she prays
> so that the goddess may gently unbind
>     her teeming womb."

It might be appropriate to adapt an ancient Roman ritual for unbinding. The man who fathered the child took off his own belt and wrapped it around the woman. Then he removed it from the woman, and spoke the line, *"se vinxisse, eundem et soluturum,"* "I have done the binding, and I will do the loosening," and then went away. If the father performed such a ritual today, he would not want to go away immediately thereafter. Moreover, a modern couple might prefer to say the line together, or to address it to God. In whatever form it takes, an unbinding ritual dramatically begins the birthing process.

Early-modern Europe (sixteenth–nineteenth centuries) made use of the symbolism of the "rose of Jericho" that pilgrims would bring back from the land of Israel. After the sourceplant tree *(anastatica hierochuntia)* has fruited, the leaves drop off and the twigs curl up to protect the ripe fruit, looking somewhat like a rose. At the start of labor, this rose was put into water, and the curled twigs would open during labor. It might be hard to get these twig balls today, but placing a real rose in hot water could also produce an opening, one that would help the birthing woman form an image of the opening of her body.

Even earlier, in Ancient Babylon, "unbinding" (for birth and other ritual reasons) was often symbolized by the peeling of an onion. An ancient prayer to the god Utu, the sun god and god of justice, prays for his help in this birth:

*This woman . . . daughter of her god;*
*may her knots be loosened before your divinity.*
*May this woman give birth in well-being.*
*Having given birth, may she live,*
*may the one inside her be well,*
*may she come in well-being before your divinity.*
*Having given birth in well-being, may she sing your praises.*

*Before your divinity may witchcraft and sorcery be loosened,*
*loosened like an onion.*
*May this woman live*

*and may she declare your greatness as long as she lives.*
*May her people know the greatness of Enki and Asarluhi*
*and may I, the incanter, your servant, sing your praises.*

# The Key Ritual

Many of the Jewish prayers have referred to the key of birthing that God holds in his hand. In European folkways, people
would bring a key from a church or synagogue for a laboring
woman to hold. Such a key, or a jewelry key that the woman
has been wearing since conception or before, could be the
centerpiece of a simple ritual in which the woman takes the
key in her hand and recites:

*Take the key of pregnancy in Your right hand*
*and open my pregnancy*
*without pain or sorrow or damage or fault.*

from the "Zera Qayyama" prayer translated on pp. 138–139 or
the following from a magical "recipe" book found in the Cairo
Genizah:

*Let it be said to Michael:*
*Take the key from your right hand . . .*
*and put it in Gabriel's left hand.*
*Let him come and open before the child (whether*
    *male or female)*
*and let it arise and praise the living God.*
*Amen amen Selah.*

# Silim-ma

The Mesopotamian unbinding prayer is a pagan hymn, to a pagan god, but the sentiments it expresses cut across religious differences. The poem survives in both Sumerian and Akkadian. It is particularly powerful in Sumerian, where one word, *silim-ma*, stands for "be well" and "in well-being." This is the word that is preserved in later languages as *shalom*. A modern monotheist version of this prayer would go:

> *silim-ma*
> *shalmish*
> *bashalom*
> *safe.*

> *I, daughter of my god,*
> *am the very gate of life.*
> *In the divine presence, I loosen the bonds upon me.*
> *May I be loose and open.*
> *May I, the woman, safely give birth.* silim-ma

> *As the onion is peeled, fold by fold, leaf by leaf,*
> *I peel off the fears and terrors surrounding me.*
> *I focus my mind only on the moment,*
> *on opening the gate of life.*
> > *May the child of my heart,*
> > *the child of my womb,*
> > *be born and be well.* silim-ma.

> *Today I stand in the Presence of God.*
> *I know the greatness of birth.*
> *The child and I stand*
> > *in the heat and light of the power.*
> *May we always come safely before You.* silim-ma

*After today I will sing Your praises,*
*I will declare Your greatness.*
*As long as I live I will declare Your greatness.*
*In awe and thanksgiving may we safely live*—silim-ma.

# The Birthing Robe

Having removed the clothing of daily existence, and loosed the knots and fastenings that symbolize both the restraints and intricacies of life in the world, the laboring woman is ready to mark her entry into the sacred realm of birth by putting on the birthing garments.

What are birthing garments? We know medieval women put on the sacred girdles of saints, but what did they wear under them? We are accustomed to wearing special clothes for special occasions: brides usually wear bridal gowns at the wedding, most ministers wear vestments during services, many Jews wear prayer shawls (tallitot) during prayer. We know what a corpse wears to its funeral, we know what a baby wears at birth, but what does a mother wear to a birthing?

This is not a trivial question. Clothes often mark the moments of our lives. We wear certain clothes to the office, others to the classroom, others for parties, still others to ball games. The clothes categorize and help identify the significance of our activities to us. They also mark our conception of ourselves and our kinship with others who are dressed the same way at the same time. The garment that we wear to a birthing also conveys messages about our culture's conception of birth.

Most women in hospitals labor and give birth in hospital gowns. They are loose and comfortable, made out of a light, sterilizable material and not too warm. But the hospital gown has serious drawbacks. The open back of a hospital gown often causes feelings of embarrassment and vulnerability. The wearer has two choices: to stay in bed so as not to expose the rear, or to wear one gown on top of another, which results in an awkward and bulky garment. But the most serious problem of the hospital gown is the message that it conveys: that the birthing mother is a patient who needs to be cared for by the hospital. This message is received by the nurses and doctors involved in the birth; it is also felt, sometimes intensely, by women who have worn the hospital gown before, at times of injury or sickness. The moment of birth—a moment of sacred power—is clouded by allusions of weakness and ill health.

As part of the return to natural childbirth, some women have begun birthing in the nude. The naked body is unconstricted and able to cool itself. Moreover, the body has been doing awesome work during pregnancy and is about to perform the magnificent act of giving birth—it should not be covered because of some sense of shame or modesty. However, this birth costume also has drawbacks. Many women do not feel at ease being naked in public, particularly if they are not giving birth at home. But again, the most important drawback about nakedness in birth is the message that it conveys: when we remove our clothes, we leave much of culture behind, we "return to nature," to enjoy physical actions like bathing, resting, sexual pleasure. Naked birth emphasizes that birth is a *natural* event. This is far more attractive than the birth-as-illness message conveyed by the hospital gown, but it is a very limited view of birth. At birth the mother steps out of ordinary time, entering the realm of the sacred, confronting the eternal presence of God in a timeless moment.

Birth is a *holy* moment. The woman enters the realm of the holy and feels the holy divine force in life as she channels her energies to deliver a new human being. Such a moment is natural, but it is also special and needs to be marked by special clothes.

It is not hard to design a birth garment. It must be loose and short, so that it does not get in the way. It should fit over the head so that it will have no fastenings, both because of the symbolism of the unbinding and so that there is nothing to become undone under strain. The sleeves should be loose and relatively short, either cap or elbow-length. Because of the symbolism of roundness, perhaps a scoop neck and cap sleeves would be appropriate. It should be made out of a lightweight fabric that can be sterilized. And it should be decorated with appropriate sayings and designs. The verse used around the cervical oval in the birth plaque, "Open for me the Righteous Gates, let me come through them and praise Yah," from Psalm 118:19, would be appropriate for the neck or the hem of such a garment. Equally meaningful, the front might be embroidered with the message that was once inscribed on the high priest's headdress: "Holy to the Lord."

The color of the garment can vary. It could be white, the color of purity and new beginnings. It could be blue, the color of the high priest's Ephod, and so often associated with Mary. It could be red, often the color of birth and of death. It could be violet, the vaginal violet that is also the international woman's color. And it could be purple, the color of royalty, whose name ARGAMAN we have seen on birth amulets as the acronym of the protecting archangels. Or it could be a rainbow of all these colors. Whatever is chosen should be colorful, festive, and glorious.

I envision two kinds of birth garments. One kind could be made out of the same cloth as hospital gowns, but different in form as they are different in function. These could be made out of a printed fabric, as are the robes worn in the nursery, and still be sterilizable. They could also be imprinted with designs relating to birth. Birthing women would then receive these garments in the hospital as patients receive their gowns, but they and their attendants would know that they were wearing them for birth and not for ill health.

Some women would not be satisfied with this and would want to make their own birthing costume, or to buy one in advance that they could embroider with these designs and keep as a treasured heirloom. An embroidered birth gown could be a gift from friends to the birthing woman or could be passed from friend to friend within a group. If the garment is homemade and designed for home birth, it might be of linen, the traditional cloth of the priests of the temple. Alternatively, it could be ready-made out of the same cloth used in the hospital version and personalized by embroidery or appliqué. Whichever version the woman chooses, she will know that she is preparing to enter the sacred realm of birth.

At some point in labor, when the room has been made sacred and the woman feels she is ready, she takes off her ordinary clothes, leaves ordinary time, and puts on this ritual garment. This is the time to think of the meaning of the garment and of the allusions it conveys. This is the moment when the woman leaves the waiting gestational period and enters a time of struggle to push a human being into this world. The woman donning her birthing robe is preparing for intense effort. She must put on strength, purpose, and dedication as she enters this sacred time.

## ENROBING

*I put on light*
>*as God put on light.*
>*God wore light as a garment*
>*and stretched out the heavens like a tent*   (Ps. 104:3)
>*at the time of earth's creation.*

*Now I wear the light of creation*
*on the day of my child's creation*
*for my child to see the light of God.*

*I put on strength*
*as God put on strength.*
*when God conquered the forces of disorder*
*and reigned over the waters*
*in the days of the world's creation.*                    (Ps. 93:1)
*I put on strength*
*as the arm of God put on strength*
*in the early days of creation*
*and on the day of Israel's redemption.*                  (Isa. 51:9)
*I put on strength*
*as Zion put on strength*
*on the day of her deliverance,*
*the day of her redemption.*                              (Isa. 52:1)
*Now I put on strength*
*on my day of struggle,*
*the time of my child's redemption.*
*May it be a day of deliverance.*

*I put on linen,*
*as the ancient priests of Israel wore linen*
*while performing sacred service.*
*Holy garments for a holy mission*
*worn in the holiest space.*
*I put on linen,*
*like the messengers of God*
*to the prophets of Israel*
*who officiated and explained*
*the moments of life and death.*
*Now I put on linen,*
*at my holiest moment of service,*

performing my holy mission
at the boundaries of life and death.

The Spirit of God moves among us,
    resting upon us,
    enveloping us with the Presence,
    entering into us at our moments of danger
    and sacred mission.

So once, the spirit of God clothed itself with     (Judges 6:43)
    Gideon,
    and he blew the shofar
    and called the people to their deliverance.
The spirit clothed itself with Amisai.
    and he came to help David struggle with     (I Chron. 12:18)
    Saul.
The Spirit clothed itself with
    Zechariah the Priest
    and he rose up to reform the people.     (2 Chron. 24:20)

I put on my sacral garment,
    but I cannot put on the spirit.
    I invoke the spirit of God
    that it clothe itself with me.

I put on a robe,
    garment of priests and kings,
    mark of leadership and divine office.
I put on adornment, like a bride,
    and splendid attire, like a warrior.     (Ezek. 23:6,12; 38:4)

God put on majesty,
    and glory and splendor

*in the days of God's creation.* (Ps. 104:3)
*God wears victory like a coat of mail*
*with a helmet of triumph on the head.* (Isa. 59:17)
*The Priests of God wear victory.* (Ps. 139:29; 2 Chron. 6:41)

*It is the day of my creation;*
*It is the day of my great battle;*
*It is the day of my own priesthood:*

"I greatly rejoice in the Lord,
    my whole being exults in God.
For he is clothing me in garments of
    triumph,
        wrapping me in a robe of victory.
Like a bridegroom adorned with a turban
    and a bride bedecked with finery." (Isa. 61:10)
*So may it be!*

# For a Speedy Delivery

Labor can be short, or it can be very long. Women have always prayed for a speedy delivery. The Sumerian myth *Enki
and Ninhursag* recalls that, long ago, goddesses had short pregnancies and gave birth very easily. When the mother goddess
Nintu/Ninhursag mated with Enki:

*She conceived the semen in the womb,*
    *the very semen of Enki,*
*But one day was her one month,*
*But two days were her two months,*
*But three days were her three months,*
*But four days were her four months,*

*But five days were her five months,*
*But six days were her six months,*
*But seven days were her seven months,*
*But eight days were her eight months,*
*But nine days were her nine months!*

*In the month of womanhood, like juniper oil,*
*like juniper oil,*
*like a prince's sweet butter*
*did Nintu, mother of the country,*
*like juniper oil*
*give birth.*

Those days were long gone by the time the Sumerians wrote this poem, which records how successive generations of goddesses gave birth this way until the goddess Uttu was born, married, and had difficulty with childbearing. We can hear the wishful thinking in this "memory" of an easier time. A modern woman might add her own postscript:

*My one month was a full month,*
*my two months were two months*
*my three months were three months*
*my nine months were nine months.*

*But in the month of motherhood, like juniper,*
*like juniper oil*
*like a prince's sweet butter,*
*like juniper oil*
*may I give birth.*

Another Mesopotamian prayer, from Babylon over a thousand years later, pictures the god Asarluhi addressing the child.

*Run hither to me like a gazelle.*
*Slip out to me like a little snake.*
*I, Asalluhi, am the midwife.*
*I will receive you.*

## Invoking Divine Aid

Women do not birth through their own power alone. Throughout pregnancy, the divine presence has helped form the child in the womb. Now this divinity is felt and longed for in the birthing chamber. The intercessory prayers traditionally said during the last months of pregnancy are also recited during labor. The patrons of childbirth—Mother Rachel, or Mary, Marguerite, and Girard are asked for their aid.

An unpublished Italian Jewish prayer book from the early eighteenth century invokes the presence of the archangel Michael for a rapid birth. It is a good prayer for the woman's partner and friends to say, perhaps while resting a hand on the woman's abdomen:

> *"Before she labored, she gave birth.*
> *Before her contractions came, she delivered*     (Isa. 66:7–8)
>     *a son."*

> *May it be your will,*
> *O Lord God of the spirits of all flesh,*
> *that you should send the angel Michael,*
>     *the one who brought the good news to Sarah*
> *and let him rest his hand*
> *on the stomach of this woman,*
> *that she may give birth in a little while*

*without the sorrows of birth,*
*that she should not take part in Eve's destiny.*
    *Amen.*

*"And your servants will come down to me*
*and bow down to me saying, 'Go out.' "*                    (Exod. 11:8)


## Reciting Famous Births

A magical recipe book from the Cairo Genizah contains this prayer-incantation that reminds the mother and God of God's ability to grant healthy births.

*Say:*
*In the beginning,*
*in the name of the living God,*
*the One who spoke and the world came to be*
*who created humans in God's image . . .*
*created them male and female.*

*And Adam knew his wife Eve*
*and she was pregnant and gave birth.*

*And Hagar bore a child to Abram*
*and called his name.*

*This is the God who remembered Sarah*
*and Sarah gave birth to a son to Abram.*

*And this is the God before whom Isaac prayed*
*and God accepted his prayer and his wife Rivka became pregnant,*
*and as her days reached the birth time*
*he came out of her and afterwards his brother.*

And this is the God who saw that Leah was unbeloved
and gave her conception and she became pregnant
and gave birth to a son and called his name.

And this is the God who remembered Rachel
and received her prayers and gave her conception
and she became pregnant and bore a son
and called his name Joseph.

As the wife of Judah gave birth,
as it is written that Judah saw there
the daughter of a Canaanite whose name was Shua
and he took her for his wife and came to her
and she became pregnant and bore a son and called his name Er.

As the man came from the house of Levi
and took a daughter of Levi
and the woman became pregnant and bore a son
and saw that he was good.

As when Moses decided to live with the man
and he gave him his daughter Zipporah to Moshe
and she bore a son and called his name Gershom,

So should _____ daughter of _____ give birth.

At this hour.
Now!
Fast!
Right away!
In an instant!

# 9. LABOR

Labor is a powerful experience. It is a time in which humans are joined by the divine, are partners to the divine, partake of divine nature, and create the divine image. It is a moment in which we confront God—a moment in which we can realize that being human involves the responsibility to be a part of God's activity, to be a part of God. Labor is a time when human social activity is integrated with the forces of nature, an event that makes us conscious that human life is intertwined with and part of a cosmic ongoing scheme. It is a biological event that can teach us that biology is spirituality, that through the body we can be one with nature, one with the cosmos. As part of nature, not as something separate from it or controlling it, we create that which we value most in nature. Birth is a profoundly sacred event, and every part of labor, the contractions, water, oil, blood, even the pain, has a spiritual significance of its own.

# Psalms of Labor

In Judaism it was also the practice to read two psalms during labor and to inscribe them on amulets. The earliest psalm to be so used is Psalm 20. There are formal reasons for its popularity for this purpose. It has nine verses: one for each month of pregnancy. Sometimes it was read nine times for magical purposes, or $9 \times 9$. But the psalm's relevance is not confined to such formal factors. It talks about the time of trouble, *tsarab*, literally, a time of narrowness or straits, a term particularly appropriate for labor. The psalm refers to victory in time of great struggle and battle, another apt metaphor for the intensity of labor. It expresses the sense that the victory is not entirely in our power, and that therefore we depend on the saving might of God. Finally, it requests that God answer and deliver and concludes with the assurance that God answers petitions.

In the following translation, I have set the psalm antiphonally, to bring out its dialogic character, labeling the parts as *W*, the woman, *O*, the other(s), and *OW* for both. In practice people who might choose actually to read the psalm during labor may want all to be read by others.

## PSALM 20

O: *On your day of trouble,*
   *YHWH answers,*
   *the name of Jacob's God defends.*

*God sends your help from the Holy place,*
   *your support from Zion.*

*God remembers all your offerings,*
*accepts your gifts,*
*grants the words of your heart,*
*fulfills your desires.*

OW: *We will rejoice in your victories,*
*set banners with the name of our God.*
*May YHWH grant all your petitions.*

W: *I know now that God rescues the anointed,*
*answers from Holy Heaven,*
*saves with the right hand of mighty deeds.*

*There are those with chariots,*
*those with horses,*
*and we—we call on the name of Yah.*
*They may kneel and fall, we stand firm.*

OW: *YHWH, save us!*
*The King answers us on the day that we*
*call.*

As time went on, Psalm 121 gained in popularity as a birthing psalm, ultimately displacing Psalm 20. It was so often written on the wall plaques that were hung to protect the mother that these plaques began to be called *Shir-hama'aloszettel,* (song-of-ascent plaques). This psalm doesn't have the battle and victory imagery of Psalm 20 and is far calmer, emphasizing God's constant supervision and protection. Once again, I have set the psalm antiphonally.

## PSALM 121

W: *To the hills I lift my eyes.*
    *Where will my help come from?*
*My help is from YHWH, who makes heaven and earth.*


O: *May God not let your foot falter,*
    *let your guardian not sleep.*
*For the guardian of Israel doesn't sleep, doesn't slumber.*
*YHWH is your guardian.*
*YHWH is your protector at your right hand.*
*By day the sun will not strike you, nor the moon at night.*
*YHWH guards you from all harm,*
    *protects your life.*
*YHWH will guard you as you go out*
    *and as you go in*
*from now till forever.*


# Labor Pains

Labor usually produces pain. A few women may have very short, easy labors or may never experience labor pains, but most labor is long, with fairly intense pain. Traditional Western religion has explained that God never intended the pain of birth but decreed it as a punishment for the misdeed of Eve. All women suffer labor pains forever for the sin of mother Eve, just as all people suffer death because of the same misdeed. This view had such a hold on Christian thinking that when analgesics began to be discovered, many Christian clergy held them to be contrary to the wishes of God as expressed in

Genesis 3 and forbade their use in childbirth. The theological debate about anesthetics continued into the middle of the nineteenth century. Moreover, the common belief that labor pains were a punishment for sin was so strong that people would even read this "curse" to women during labor. A good example of this attitude toward labor pains is this French "Prayer of the Pregnant Woman Awaiting her Confinement," from the seventeenth and eighteenth centuries.

> *In my confinement, strengthen my heart to endure the pains that come therewith, and let me accept them as the consequence of your judgment upon our sex, for the sin of the first woman. In view of that curse, and of my own offenses in marriage, may I suffer the cruelest pangs with joy, and may I join them with the sufferings of your Son upon the cross, in the midst of which He engendered me into eternal life. Never can they be as harsh as I deserve, for although holy matrimony has made my conception legitimate, I confess that concupiscence mingled its venom therewith and that it has urged me to commit faults which displease you. If it be your will that I die in my confinement, may I adore it, bless it and submit to it.*

In this prayer, the woman accepts her pain as punishment for her sins, both hers personally and those of Eve. Such an attitude totally separates the experience of birth pains from all other experiences of suffering. It also blames the victim. But, as the Biblical book of Job makes very clear, the sufferer may be totally innocent of wrongdoing, and it is wrong to blame a sufferer for his or her own suffering. Our religious traditions have given us a double message: they have taught us not to blame the sufferer and not to assume that pain or hardship come as punishment, but at the same time, some of these same traditions have blamed women for their labor pains.

Perhaps in rebellion against the concept of pain as punishment or as sacrifice, women in the nineteenth century began to rebel against the very experience of labor pain by the formation of a mass movement, the Twilight Sleep movement, which demanded total anesthesia for women so that they would not experience pain. This was, in its day, a feminist demand, but when it succeeded in making Twilight Sleep a common feature of birth in the mid-twentieth century, it had the effect of totally robbing women of the experience of childbirth. In removing their pain, it also removed their participation and memory of the event and made them the passive recipients of the ministrations of the birth attendant. The doctor "delivered" the baby; the woman "was delivered" of the child.

The move toward more natural childbirth has returned birth to women. Instead of obliterating consciousness, the modern methods of birth like Lamaze and Bradley attempt to teach women how to manage their breathing and body processes so that they do not feel the pain. These methods cannot eliminate pain, however; and all too frequently, women who have been prepared for natural childbirth are dismayed when they feel pain and may think that it is a sign that something is wrong. As a result, their bodies may try to suppress the pain, thus inadvertently slowing down their contractions. The result is a medicated birth and an unfortunate sense of guilt and failure by the mother.

Pain cannot be avoided in childbirth. It is neither a sign of distress nor of punishment. Rather, it is the body's experience of the tremendous physical effort of giving birth.

A passage from Isaiah refers to the inevitability of childbirth pain:

> *Before she could labor, she gave birth;*
> *before her pangs could come upon her,*
> *    she delivered a boy-child.*

*Who ever heard of such a thing?*
*Who ever saw such as this?*
*Can the earth create in one day?*
*Can a nation be born in an instant?*
*Zion is in labor—*
*and she will bear her children.*

Here the laboring woman is not a daughter of Eve. She is Zion, the mystical figure of the city of Jerusalem portrayed as a woman. Her labor is not the result of a fall from grace, not a sign of sin. If anything, it is the greatness of the product that demands the intensity of the act.

The Book of Revelation has another image of a cosmic female in birth pangs:

*And a great portent appeared in heaven*
*A woman clothed with the sun,*
*with the moon under her feet*
*and on her head a crown of twelve stars—*
*She was with child*
*And she cried out in her pangs of birth*
*in anguish for delivery.*

The great city of Zion, the cosmic heavenly woman of Revelation, and human women labor and endure pain to birth life. Animals usually do not. Labor in food production and labor in childbirth are the two great characteristics of human beings in which our difference from the animal world is manifest. Most animals do not have to work for food, clothing, and shelter, and even those animals who do work (like beavers and birds) do so basically only for their own immediate needs. Similarly, most animals do not have difficult births. God's pronouncement in Genesis 3 is a predictive description of the nature of human life, not an expression of punitive action. By eating the fruit of the tree of knowledge, humans left the natural animal order of simplicity and entered the more turbulent world of wisdom and culture. They became quintessentially human. But there is a price to pay. The world of culture, with its greater demands, cannot be sustained without great effort, and beings of culture cannot come into being without the same type of intense effort. This gives rise to the pain in human births.

Scientific investigation leads to the same conclusion. The upright posture of early humans was accompanied by a progressive rigidification and narrowing of the pelvic structure. At the same time, it allowed intellectual development. This demanded a larger cranial size at birth. While the pelvic opening was getting smaller, the head of the fetus was getting larger. This results in the classic cephalo-pelvic disproportion which demands labor and labor and more labor in order to stretch the cervix to its maximum and thereby force open the passageway so that the baby's head can fit through. All that effort to dilate is indeed a consequence of the step in human development that produced a sophisticated creator who has "eaten of the fruit of knowledge."

The French birth prayer just quoted also hints at another philosophy of birth pains, that they are akin to the sufferings of Jesus on the cross. The Passion has been an important symbol of pain in Christian thought and has enabled sufferers to feel that they walk in the ways of God, not despite their suffering, but even because of it. Moreover, in classic Christian thought, the Passion of the crucifixion brought humanity into new life. The similarity of this pain-birth combination to childbirth is first expressed by Bishop Anselm of Canterbury:

> You have died more than they, that they may labor to bear. It is by
> your death that they have been born, for if you had not been in labor,
> you could not have borne death; and if you had not died, you would

*not have brought forth. For, longing to bear sons into life, You tasted
death, and by dying, you begot them.*

The image of Jesus as a laboring mother is expressed most
fully in the writings of Julian of Norwich:

*But our true Mother, Jesus, he alone bears us for joy and for endless
life, blessed may he be. So he carries us within him in love and
travail, until the full time when he wanted to suffer the sharpest thorns
and cruel pains that ever were or will be, and at the last he died. And
when he had finished, and had borne us so for bliss, still all this could
not satisfy his wonderful love.*

The parallel between Jesus' suffering and birth pangs emphasizes the motherly birth-bearing aspect of Jesus' mission.
At the same time, it takes the birth pangs of the mother out of
the realm of sin and punishment and into the category of
suffering in order to achieve something, particularly for others. The nearness of the God who suffers is also prominent in
modern Christian reflections on the birth experience. Léonie
Caldecott comes to her birthing as a religious Catholic, rosary
between her fingers and icon of Our Lady of Czestochowa as
a focal point. As the pains continue, "I catch the sad eyes of
the Czestochowa icon. Behind the image of mother and child,
another figure looms. The Crucified Christ." So, too, Margaret
Hammer relates how she tried to focus her breathing and
prayers by visualizing a peaceful risen Christ or Mary throned
in glory, only to find that all she could see "was Jesus on a
cross, struggling for every breath." She suggests a simple
prayer to help in breathing during labor: "**Lord Jesus Christ,
who gave birth on the cross, bless us as we labor.**"

The work and pain of labor are marks of our humanity.
Insects do not labor, nor birds, nor even, usually, the other
mammals. Moreover, human women are in very privileged

company in their labor pains, the company of the Holy and the Sacred. Mother Zion labors, she "writhes and pants." The world itself must go through the "birth pangs of the Messiah" in order to bring the new order of the Messianic days. And even God is like a laboring woman as God creates the new order: "Now I will scream like a woman in labor, I will pant and I will gasp." The very significance of the birth—a human, not a bee—demands great effort in its production.

We would like a world of sweetness and light, but such is not reality. The real world can neither come into being nor exist without effort and struggle, and this world involves pain. Ancient myth and biblical poetry relate that God had to struggle against the forces of chaos before the world could come into being. Before law came the flood; before deliverance from Egypt, the plagues; before the settlement, the conquest; before the restoration, the exile. This pattern has continued in human history, as every new age has been birthed by a harsh destruction of the old. And, we are told, it will continue in the future as Armageddon precedes the eschaton. Before creation, the old must be destroyed and a tremendous effort must be sustained. This painful process fuels both history and biography, creating the rhythm of our world.

### THE HYMN OF PAIN

*First the pain and then the progress.*
*First the trial, then the peace.*
*Turmoil, torment, suffering, and anger,*
*is this the way deliverance begins?*

*Into the stillness of the beginning*
*came the turmoil of mighty waters.*

*Chaos unleashed, disaster unbounded,*
*then, at last, "YHWH is king!"*

*Ten disasters came upon Egypt,*
*plagues and pestilence and doom.*
*Amidst the tragedy there is a purpose,*
*birthing Israel to set it free.*

*Floods and exiles, disasters and wars,*
*Revolutions and bloodbaths and riots.*
*Each age passes to the next one,*
*hoping the future will redeem.*

*From the ashes rises the Phoenix.*
*Does Crucifixion lead to Salvation?*
*After the Holocaust came the State . . .*
*Will this pattern someday end?*

*Today is the day of my creation,*
*A whole new world comes into being.*
*I can be strong enough to birth it,*
*only pray I do not bear wind.* (Isa. 26:18)

It is important to realize that the pains of birth are part of
the cosmic pattern. They are not specially inflicted on women,
neither as punishment nor as an opportunity for glory. The
laboring woman is neither a victim nor a martyr. Discerning
this cosmic pattern of creation locates the difficulty of childbirth in this universal pattern. Instead of being an occasion for
guilt or concern, it becomes a signifier of the tremendous act
of creation involved in giving birth.

Religions have long tried to understand suffering in the
universe. Beyond the notions of suffering as punishment (re-
jected except for birth pain) have come ideas of suffering as

redemption and suffering as refinement or education. The suffering of a few has been perceived as payment for the misdeeds of the many. More often, the suffering has been perceived as the way that humanity learns and improves. Today these interpretations do not find many adherents, for they do not match our current ethical ideas or theories of education. Pain is not always a path to learning, and the infliction of corporal punishment may teach only that might makes right.

The pain of childbirth labor has some positive aspects. It prevents us from taking birth casually. It makes people deeply conscious of the present moment; in labor it causes women to be mindful of the process of birth, to confront their deepest beliefs, and to mobilize their strengths and resources to work through the pain and for birth. It reminds us of our limits even as we move to transcend them. Above all, it prevents people from totally spiritualizing the birth and the baby. Humans are embodied beings. Our bodies are important and part of our essence. We experience life through our bodies, with all the pain, illness, struggle, and well-being that they bring us. Birth is an event, an achievement of the body in which another body is expelled and brought to independent existence. It is a supreme body experience, and the pain brings women more fully into their bodies, ready to feel both the effort and the ecstasy with all their being.

# Contractions

During labor, the whole body of the birthing woman convulses in the effort to birth the child. The often violent motion of the mother has been a frequent metaphor for extreme agitation. The Bible speaks many times of people having experiences "like a woman giving birth." They suffer pangs like her, and most often they quake with *hil kayoleda*, "shaking like a woman giving birth." When we look carefully to see which experiences are compared to birth tremors, then we begin to see the deeper meaning of these contractions.

## LIKE A BIRTHING WOMAN

*On coming to Jerusalem, kings stand in wonder*
    *trembling seizes them*—hil kayoleda     (Ps. 48:7)

*It is not the stone that is astonishing*
    *Babylon is bigger*
    *Nineveh is stronger*
    *Rome is more powerful.*

*It is the nearness of the Presence*
    *the greatness of the Presence*
    *the awesome might of God*—hil kayoleda.     (Ps. 48:7)

*Today—a sudden tightening,*
*my body shakes,*
*my fingers tremble.*
*The time has come.*

*On the high mountain of my pain I climb,*
*I who brings glad tidings.*
*I lift my voice with strength,*
*I cry aloud,*
    *Behold our God!*     (Isa. 40:9)

*Sound the trumpet, for I hear the rushing of a*
    *mighty force.*

*I howl: the divine day is at hand.*　　　　　　　　　　(Isa. 13:4–9)
*The coming of the Lord shakes the earth—*
　　　*shakes the people,*
　　　*shakes the soul.*
*We howl, we quake, our faces flame.*
*We feel the power of the divine host.*
*My hands grow limp,*
*my heart is trembling,*
*pangs and throes—*hil kayoleda.

*It is in battle that men have felt this power,*
*felt the trembling,*
*the coming of God,*
*the danger and the glory of the cosmic forces.*

*Sound the trumpet, they have called.*
*Sound the alarm!*
*The day of the Lord comes and is near.*　　　　　　　(Joel 2:6)
*The nations tremble,*
*the hills tremble,*
*the earth shakes.*
*A mighty force is coming.*
*The men of Israel heard,*
*the king of Babylon heard the mighty hordes.*
*His hands also trembled—*hil kayoleda

*Scream! for I, too, hear the sound of mighty*
　　　*combat.*
*The battle is on!*
*The forces near!*
*Like a rocking war chariot,*
*like a bucking plow,*
*I feel the movement,*
*the heat,*

*the sweat,*
*the dust of battles swirls around me.*
*I feel the coming of God's mighty force.*
*I tremble and quake—hil kayoleda.*

*A mighty force is coming,*
*in awe, in terror,*
*I pray that I will not bear wind,*       (Isa. 26:18)
*that the child can bear the battle,*       (Hos. 13:13)
*that in the wake of this great coming,*
*God will leave our blessing.*
*And in the terror and the struggle of this great*
    *battle,*
*I work for life.*

# Noise

Western culture has many inhibitions against women making noise. It is not "ladylike" to speak too loudly, it is not "refined" to laugh loudly, it is never appropriate to scream. Women who have been socialized to accept these premises often try to have a silent labor and may worry in advance that they will "lose control" and behave in an "uncivilized manner." But labor is not a time for silence. It is a time for release, for pants and groans and screams. The Sumerian incantations have a set formula to indicate that a woman has begun labor: "Her cries reached heaven, her cries reached earth." In a magical "recipe" book found in the Cairo Genizah, we read the following incantation to be recited over water in the event of difficulty in childbirth:

*A Heavenly Voice comes up from the earth to the heavens*
*and says before the living God:*
*The sound . . . (is) not the sound of mountains overturning . . .*
*but the sound of Mme X daughter of X.*
*Answer her, please, in this hour.*

The noise of a laboring woman has many roles. It expresses her distress, it petitions for help, and it increases her ability to cope with pain. It is the announcing of struggle, like the shout of soldiers and the blowing of trumpets. It is the auditory component of struggle and concentration, like the cry of a karate master. It is a demand for help, a cry to call attention and await an answer. And it is the sound of strength, as the day of the Lord arrives and God roars through us. Rather than bid a laboring woman to be silent, we should blow trumpets to accompany the labor.

## SHOUT

### ša'ag: *The Roaring*

*It is the time of roaring.*
*I roar in my distress,* (Ps. 38:9)
*I roar all day,* (Ps. 32:3)
*and my roars seem far from redemption.* (Ps. 22:2)

*God roars,*
*like a lion roaring in strength,* (Hosea 11:10)
*coming in battle,* (Amos 3:8; Isa. 5:29)
*doing divine wonders.* (Job 37:4–5)

*Wherever God is, God roars.*
*God roars from the skies, God's holy habitation.*   (Jer. 25:30)
*God roars from Zion, gives voice from Jerusalem.*   (Amos 1:2)

*Today God roars through me, God's dwelling seat.*
*God roars through me, who have become like*
    *Jerusalem.*
*The sound of God's voice shakes me, shakes the*
    *earth.*
*May this roaring be near to redemption.*

## tsa'aq: *The Cry*

*I cry out to the Lord to answer me.*
*I cry to God as the prophets of old.*
*Hear me and respond!*
*Once you heard the cry of Moses:*
*frogs were removed,*                        (Ex 8:8)
*bitter waters became sweet,*                (Ex 15:25)
*and Miriam was healed*                      (Num 11:12)
*So I cry to you:*
*preserve my child!*
*You delivered Israel when they cried unto you,*
*you delivered them from Egypt,*      (Ex 3:7; 14:10; Num 20:16)
*delivered them from Canaanites,*            (Judg. 4:3)
*delivered them from Chaos.*                 (1 Sam. 9:16)
*Deliver now my child!*

*I cry out to the Lord to demand what is mine,*
*as the Shunnemite cried out before the king,*   (2K 8:3,5)
*I cry out to demand what is mine to demand,*
*Give my child to me!*

I cry out to the Lord in the time of my distress,     (Exod. 22:22, 26)
for God listens to those in distress.
"My voice is to God and I shout.
My voice is to the Lord.
Listen to me in the time of my distress."     (Ps. 77:2)
"The Lord my God is my salvation by day,
my cry comes before you at night."     (Ps. 88:2)
"They cry unto God who hears
and saves them from all their straits."     (Ps. 34:18)
I cry out to the Lord in my straits,
and God will answer me expansively.     (Ps. 118:5)

## tru'ah: The Shouting

The priests of Israel had two silver trumpets,
and sent up sound to the very heaven—     (Num. 10:5–6)
a call to arms, a reminder to God—     (Num 10:9)
trumpets and shouts at the time of war.     (Num 31:6)
The trumpets sounded, the people shouted,
down came the walls of Jericho     (Josh 6:20)
I shout the shouts of struggle and war.     (Amos 1:14)
The day of the Lord is here,     (Zeph 1:14)
"Blow the trumpets in Zion and shout on my holy
    mount,
the day of the Lord is coming, it is very near."     (Joel 2:1)
The shouts reach to heaven, spread throughout
    earth
heralding victory and success.
When Judah shouted, God defeated Jeroboam.     (1 Chron. 13:12, 15)
The walls of Babylon will not withstand the
    shouts of Israel.     (Jer. 50:15)
Today to my shouts, the walls of my body shake
    and part.

## tsarah: *The Scream*

A new world begins with screams and with tumult:
"God goes out like a man of war
shouting and screaming, subduing all enemies."          (Isa. 42:13)
I hear the screams: are they mine or God's?
Today I, the warrior,
am shouting and screaming,
crying in fear, in struggle and strength.
Today is the day a new world comes to be,
a new human being is being born.

A new world begins with gasps and with roaring:
"As a laboring woman, God blows, pants and
    breathes."          (Isa. 42:14)
The sound of God's blowing fills the earth,
powerful gusts shaking all before them,
leading the blind in a way they do not know,
marching them on unfamiliar paths,
turning the darkness into light          (Isa. 42:14–16)
coming to level ground.

Today I, a woman, am laboring,
filling the world with my cries,
bringing my child on paths unfamiliar
redeeming my child from darkness to light.

Hear my cry!

I cry in pain,
I cry in anger,
I cry in supplication,
in strength and in struggle.
My piercing cry can become a lament or a shout of
    joy.

*The answer is in your hands, God.*
*Hear my cry,*
*work with me to deliver life*
*and I shall lift my voice to the sky in jubilation.*


# Answer Me!


People who call want God to answer, and Judaism has developed liturgical forms to call for such aid, based on the word *'anah*, "answer." The simplest uses the word *anenu*, "answer us," followed by epithets of God. This form is found in the liturgy for the holiday of Shmini Atseret. It is also used in personal piety. One of the texts of "Zera Qayyama" (pp. 138–139) prescribes that the couple say two Anenu litanies before they recite this prayer. An example of such a litany used at the time of labor is included in Bela Yudita's prayer book, with *anenu* "answer us," changed to *aneni*, "answer me." The prayer reads:

*Answer me, God of Abraham, answer me.*
*Answer me, Dread of Isaac, answer me.*
*Answer me, Great One of Jacob, answer me.*
*Answer me, Lord of Mercy and Forgiveness, answer*
  *me.*
*Answer me, the one who answers laboring women*
  *on the birth stool, answer me.*
*Answer me, the one who saves from destruction and*
  *gives life to the dead, answer me.*
*Answer me, the one who takes note of barren women*
  *and opens the wombs, answer me.*

*May the King of the King of Kings*
*who heard and answered the prayers*
　　*of the holy and pure mothers*
　　*who were by nature barren,*
*and changed their condition for the better,*
*and looked after them in mercy,*
　　*from the long and wide mercy seat,*
*and they were regarded and remembered with human*
　　*seed;*
*may God regard and remember me for good,*
*for mercy and lovingkindness*
*at this time that I pray.*

The most famous "answer me" prayer litany is recited by the whole community. It was written during the first century and is still recited during the penitential prayers before the New Year. This consists of seven benedictions in the form "May the one who answered X answer you and hear your cries today. Blessed are you God, who . . ." And the figures whose prayers God answered were Abraham, the Israelites at the Red Sea, Joshua, Samuel, Elijah, Jonah, and David and Solomon.

Two medieval midrashim indicate that this formula was also used in personal piety and, in particular, for pregnancy. The midrashim are comments on Psalm 20:2—"The Lord answers you in times of straits." *Deuteronomy Rabbah* asks, "The Lord answers you in the day of trouble"—What is the meaning of "the day of trouble?" Resh Lakish said, just as, when a woman in labor is seated in the birthing chair, people say to her, "May the one who answered your mother answer you," so said David to Israel, "He who answered Jacob, he will answer you." A fuller form of this formula is preserved in *Midrash Tehillim*, which records that when a pregnant woman has difficulty giving birth, they say to her:

lyt 'nn ywd'un mh n'mr lk, 'l' m'n d'ny l'mk bywdn qw-šyyth, hw' y'ny ytk b'ydn qšywtk, *"we don't know what to say to you, but the one who answered your mother at the time of her troubles, he will answer you at the time of your troubles."*

This formula is in Aramaic, and was probably very old by the time it was quoted in the midrash. Another Aramaic formula is preserved in *Midrash Tehillim,* commenting on Psalm 20:

*There are nine verses in this psalm, corresponding to the nine months that a woman is pregnant with a child. And what do they say: m'an d'h' 'lehyyt' 'l mtbr', hw' y'ny ytkwn, "the one who answers the pregnant woman during labor, he will answer you."*

Using these ancient formulas, I have composed a modern petitionary litany for childbirth. The form of the individual stanzas is that of the standard litany. Each stanza has been provided with an antiphon, "howl!" which is based on the full preserved description of this litany. After each benediction was recited by the reader, the assembled congregation answered, "Blessed be His glorious majesty forever" in the days when the temple still stood, and after its destruction the congregation answered "amen." The sexton then turned to the priests and called, "Shout, O sons of Aaron, shout," and we assume the priests shouted before the next benediction was recited. Instead of seven benedictions, I include ten, as an appropriate number for pregnancy and in order to include some traditional statements of this form that have been preserved in Jewish prayers.

## ANENI

*In times of trouble we call upon You,*
*shouting, lifting our cries to the sky,*
*covering earth with our screams.*
*Pay attention! Pay heed! Answer me now!*
*And in the very moment of the scream,*
*I long for and bless the answer.*

*I recite the benedictions of supplication:*

rahamana di ʿaneh letvirey libba, ʿaneni.
*The merciful One who answers the broken of heart,*
        *answer me!*

mʾan dʿaneʾ lehayyataʾ ʿal mitbaraʾ, hwʾ
        yaʿany yatkwn.
*May the One who answers the pregnant woman*
        *during labor answer you.*

maʾn daʿney leʾimak bywdn qwšayyatah, hwʾ
        yaʿney yatak bʾydan qašywtak.
*May the One who answered your mother at the*
        *time of her troubles answer you at the time of*
        *your troubles.*

*May the One who answered your mother*
        *at the time of her troubles*
    *answer you and hear your shouts today.*
    *We bless You, our redeemer.*
                        *Howl, O woman.*

*May the One who answered Sarah*
        *in the sorrow of her barrenness*          (Gen. 21:1)

answer you and hear your shouts today.
we bless You, who paid heed to Sarah.
                    Scream, O daughter of Eve.


May the One who answered Hagar
        in the anguish of the desert,          (Gen. 21:16–19)
answer you and hear your shouts today.
We bless You, who remembers the forgotten.
                    Howl, O woman.


May the One who answered Rebekkah
        at the moment of her plea          (Gen. 25:22)
answer you and hear your shouts today.
We bless You, who listens to petitions.
                    Lift your voice and shout.


May the One who answered Rahab
        at the moment of her loyalty          (Josh. 22)
answer you and hear your shouts today.
We bless You, who listens to shouts.
                    Fill heaven with cries!


May the One who answered Deborah
        at the moment of her strength          (Judg. 4, 5)
answer you and hear your shouts today.
We bless You, who listens to screams.
                    Howl, O woman.


May the One who answered Hannah
        in the temple of Shiloh          (1 Sam. 1)
answer you and hear your shouts today.
We bless You, who listens to prayers.
                    Howl, woman.

*May the One who answered Jonah*
  *in the belly of the fish*      (Jonah 2)
  *answer you and hear your shouts today.*
  *We bless You, who answers in time of crisis.*
             *Howl!*

*May the One who answered David*
  *in the time of his distress*      (Ps. 20:2)
  *answer you and hear your shouts today.*
  *We bless You, who answers on the day that*
  *we call.*
          *Make noise unto God!*

*May the One who answered our holy mothers,*
  *Sara, Rivka, Rachel, Leah and Hannah,*
  *and all the righteous proper and pious women*
  *answer you and hear your shouts today.*
*We bless you, who remembers women in labor.*
            *Shout!*

*The howling is my voice that calls its prayer and*
  *anguish.*
*May the One who answers those in crisis hear my*
  *voice.*
*May the One who answers women in labor answer*
  *me today.*

# The Oil of Birth

We bring oil to childbirth. From ancient Sumer to modern childbirth, people have anointed the birthing mother with oil. A woman rubbed with oil feels good, feels loved. Tensed muscles relax under the massage, the spirit responds to the friendly touch, the leathery pelvis grows more elastic, the cervix and vulva become more malleable.

Beyond the utilitarian purpose of the oil, everything that comes in contact with an occasion as holy as childbirth becomes holy itself. The oil is transformed by its function. It is no longer ordinary oil that can be used for everything. It is sacred oil, made sacred by its purpose. Its uniqueness may be marked by a special formula for mixing the oil with other substances or enhancing the oil with spices. Most importantly, the oil will be marked by the associations of the oil with sacred, mythical events.

In Mesopotamia, the oil was accompanied by a narrative story about a cow named Geme-$^d$Sin ("the servant of the god Suen"). This is a very special cow, for the god Nanna-Su'en fell in love with her. He placed her at the head of the herd, pastured her, gave her to drink, and impregnated her. When the days of her pregnancy were completed, she knelt to deliver. But something was wrong; the birth did not come easily, and she screamed in her labor pains. Her screams reached heaven, where the god Su'en heard her and sent help. Two female spirits came down from heaven, one carrying "oil from a jar," the other "water of labor." The two main versions differ slightly at this point; together they give us a clear picture of what is happening. The earlier text, from the middle Assyrian period, reads:

> Two are the daughters of Anu,
>> they came down from heaven.
> One was carrying "The water of labor,"
>> the second carried "oil from a jar."
> May he [the attendant] touch the water of labor to her
>> forehead; [place] the oil from the jar over all her body.
> Just as Gi-sin the servant of Sin gave birth safely,
>> so let the laboring woman give birth.

This elliptical text clearly indicates that the story accompanies a ritual in which the attendant rubs the woman with oil. The later text (KAR 196+BAM 238) is more elaborate:

> Two protective genies came down from heaven.
> One was carrying oil from a jar,
>> the other brought down the water of labor.
> She touched the oil from a jar to her forehead,
>> she sprinkled her whole body with the water of labor.
> A second time she touched the oil from a jar to her forehead,
>> she sprinkled her whole body with the water of labor.
> As she touched her the third time,
> the calf fell to the ground like a gazelle young.
>> She called the calf "milk-cow."
> Just as Geme-Sin gave birth safely,
>> so may the laboring woman give birth.
> May the midwife not be held back.
> Let the pregnant woman be safe.

In this text, the oil is placed only on the forehead. However, this later text is on a tablet that also contains another "Cow of Sin" incantation, one accompanied by a ritual in which an ointment is prepared by mixing oil with dust from a crossroads. This oil is then rubbed on the belly of the laboring woman.

This story seems a little strange to us, for we do not have a veneration of cows, nor religious associations of a bovine form. The ancient Near Eastern world did, however, and in Mesopotamia, the horns of the crescent moon were often seen as the horns of Nanna-Su'en, the god of the moon. He was also the patron god of the city of Ur and very important to the kings of the Ur III dynasty. Geme-Su'en, "servant maid of Su'en," was the name of the wife of Shulgi, king of Ur, and their son was named Amar-Sin, "calf of Sin." It has been suggested that this story about the cow, maid of Sin, who gave birth to a calf was composed for use during the queen's labor. The continuing importance of the moon-god Nanna-Su'en throughout Mesopotamian history and the hornlike appearance of the crescent moon over that region could account for the continued use of this incantation.

Today, oil cannot be placed in a sacred context by means of its associations with the birth of the calf of Su'en. But the practice of anointing the mother's pelvis with oil, now being newly rediscovered, is an old one and is known from the nineteenth-century American frontier. In some cases, it served both as the medium of and the measurement of the bonding of women. In a letter to her daughter a mother advises rubbing olive oil over the abdomen and perineal area but worries who could do it: "I don't know if you have a person you could let do it, but I wish I were there to do it." It could also be an occasion for religious invocation and blessing. Penned into the minutes of a Relief Society for the Church of Jesus Christ of Latter-Day Saints is a prayer to be said while washing and anointing the mother:

*We wash you preparatory to your safe delivery and speedy recovery*

*for Life, health, salvation*
*for yourself and your offspring,*
*asking God the Eternal Father*
*that His holy spirit may attend this ordinance.*

*That every cord and muscle may be strong and healthy,*
*that the marrow of your bones [be] warmed by the spirit of*
  *God . . .*
*that your heart might be comforted,*
*and that no cold might settle upon [your] bosom,*
*and that your milk may be pure and filled with nourishment.*

*That [your womb] might be strengthened*
*and the ligaments thereof,*
*that it may retain what is therein deposited*
*to its full time*
*and bring forth in perfection.*

*We ask that your child might be perfect*
*in every limb and joint and muscle,*
*that it might be beautiful to look upon,*
*that its nerves may be strong,*
*that it may be happy in its spirit . . .*
*that it may be free from spot or blemish,*
*that it may be filled with faith from its mother's womb.*

The Bible has many allusions to the use of oil in anointing. It sanctifies the holy and consecrates priests, prophets, and kings.

## SACRED PLACE, SACRED WOMAN

*In Ancient Israel there was a special oil,*
    *fragrant olive oil*
*spiced with cinnamon, cassia, and myrrh.*
*With this oil they made ready the holy,*
    *consecrated the sacred,*
    *anointed the holiest of all.*
*A sacred oil, sacred to God through the ages.*


*Moses took the oil and sanctified the tabernacle.*
*Seven times he sprinkled the oil on the altar and*
    *anointed it.*
*Seven times he sprinkled its vessels, its utensils.*     (Lev. 8:10–12)
*With spiced oil the holy precincts were anointed.*


*The sacred oil is the oil of priests.*
*Moses poured oil on Aaron and his sons,*     (Lev. 8:12; Num. 71–72)
*anointing them for holy service.*


*The priest stood in God's presence,*
*dwelling in the sacred realm*
*close to God, close to the people.*
*The High priest, anointed with the oil of God,*
*stayed in the realm of the Holy.*     (Lev. 21:12)
*Today we stand in the sacred realm of God,*
*feeling God's presence,*
*doing God's work.*
*You bring us into God's presence,*
*you labor to do God's work.*
*In honor of your holy action,*
*in honor of your sacred purpose,*

*in honor of your priestly essence,*
*I anoint your head today.*

*I anoint your belly, holy Tabernacle,*
*I anoint your head, holy Person,*
*I anoint your vulva, sacred portal.*
*Person, Place and Passage,*
*I anoint you today.*

# Oil for the One That Comes

The most dramatic connotation of oil in the Bible is the anointing of the "Messiah," which means "the anointed one." As the kings and priests of ancient Israel were anointed, the image of "anointed" refers to the coming leaders who will bring redemption and salvation. Deutero-Isaiah applies this term *Messiah* to Cyrus the Great of Persia, and Zachariah speaks of the "two of oil" (the priest and king). Ultimately, "the Messiah" comes to refer to the future Davidic King, who, of course, many Christians believe to have been Jesus. But, as we have seen before, each new baby is the incarnation, each child bears the name of God, and each child is the one who comes and must repair the world. It is fitting, then, that each new child be anointed.

*Come through the oiled anointed gates*
*and be anointed, child!*
*Be anointed as the priests of long ago,*
*consecrated in holiness,*
*devoted to God's service.*
*There are no High priests for us today,*
*no one to guide us in the realm of the Holy.*

We stand together in the presence of the One,
and you too must take your place in the presence of
    God.

You too must serve God in our world
and make it the holiest of dwelling places.

Today you will be anointed
    as Aaron and his sons were anointed,
    as the priests of Israel were anointed,
    as the prophet Elisha was anointed.
In the anointing is the consecration:
a touch of holiness, a connection with the sacred.
You are already holy—
may the oil that touches you declare your holiness
and remind us of the holiness in us.

Come through the oiled anointed Gates
and be anointed, child!
Be anointed as the kings of long ago,
leaders appointed by God and people
anointed in God's service.

Today, you will be anointed
    as Saul was anointed,
    as David was anointed,
    as Solomon was anointed,
    as Hazael king of Aram was anointed,
    as Cyrus king of Persia was anointed.
In the anointing is the mission,
a message of the duty of the ruler:
"The spirit of the Lord God be upon you,

because the Lord has anointed you.
He sends you as a herald of good tidings to the
        poor,
to bind up the wounded of heart,
to proclaim release to captives,
liberation to the oppressed." (Isa. 61:1)


In you are the priest, the king, and the prophet,
the tasks of all are merged in you.
May God keep faith with the anointed, (Ps. 128:15)
and be a stronghold for the deliverance of the
        anointed. (Ps. 28:8)
May God deal graciously with the anointed (2 Sam. 22:51)
        forever.


Anointed child, always remember:
As you are anointed today
so too all people are anointed,
        on the day they come out of their mother.
Never raise a hand against the Lord's anointed. (1 Sam. 24:12)
Never do violence to them.
Dare not to kill any of the Lord's anointed,
But watch over them forever.


I anoint you, mother and child,
the one who works and the one who comes.
In this most sacred of moments,
in this most sacred of places,
I anoint you with oil to mark the sacred.
May the holiness of this moment
spread out to produce
the Holiness of life.

# Water

At some point in labor comes a rush of waters, the waters of the amniotic sac in which the baby has floated like a space explorer, tethered to the mother, afloat in an ocean of liquid. When the waters break, they become a river, bearing the baby to birth. This imagery gave rise in Sumerian literature to an elaborate set of incantations meant to be recited during prolonged labor. In these texts, the mother, rolling and heaving in labor, is represented as a great boat that brings the baby along the mighty river. The boat comes from a far and distant place, for it is loaded with lapis lazuli or carnelian, both precious stones that come from the edges of the world. The mother-boat doesn't know which precious cargo she is carrying, for she doesn't know whether the baby is a boy or a girl. The mother unfurls her sails and begins her journey, but the boat gets stuck. The baby is still tethered to its original moorings, where it is described as stuck at the quay of death. It cannot pass the great ocean that separates the world of the nonalive from the world of the living. This is the deep infernal body of water over which we come and over which we go at our death. But the baby cannot reach the quay of life; the doors are stuck and will not open.

The incantations describe how one god, Asarluhi, keeps his eyes on humankind and sees the woman and the baby in their distress. He goes to the great god Enki, god of wisdom, god of magic, and god of the deepest waters, and relates to Enki the sad state of the woman and child. Enki then prescribes a ritual for the priest to perform, a ritual that will help bring about the birth, and the priest performing the ritual offers prayers that the baby will complete its journey, that the waters of birth will flow like water from a broken pot.

In these Sumerian incantations, the birth boat travels on

the cosmic waters from the very depths of the earth itself. The Bible also locates the womb of the mother as the nethermost portions of the earth: "My frame was not hidden from You when I was shaped in a hidden place, knit together in the recesses of the earth" (Psalm 139:15). This image of the birth boat, with its powerful narrative and prayer, was frequently copied and referred to in Sumerian literature and had a long life in Mesopotamia, surviving also in Akkadian versions. What follows is not an exact translation but my own adaptation of the themes of these prayers:

### SAILING TO BIRTH

*Now comes the final voyage,*
*the journey without.*
*From the center of the world,*
*from the land of the not-yet-born,*
*from the midst of the mother,*
*the journey begins.*

*The boat is full,*
*packed with treasure:*
*carnelian,*
*lapis lazuli,*
*perfume,*
*cedar wood.*
*Greatest of all cargos,*
*full to stretching,*
*the child is ready.*

*I feel the ocean wind unfurl my sails,*
*I stretch to heaven, stretch to earth.*
*My cries reach heaven, reach to earth,*

*I rise and fall like a roiling ocean,*
*I pitch and rock like a ship in a storm.*

*And in me the boat,*
*the processional boat,*
*the precious baby boat,*
*starts its journey.*

*It leaves its moorings,*
*leaves the safe haven that suits it no more.*
*Now is the danger:*
*the dock of growth, of nurture,*
*may become the quay of death.*

*Open wide the great gate,*
*as the boat sails free to birth.*
*"May the waters flow like rain,*
*may they flow like water from a pail,*
*may (the boat) break like a broken pot."*
*as it reaches the land of life.*

Water's associations are not limited to the sailing of boats:

## THE WATERS

*Over the waters hovers the spirit.*
*So began the life of the world,*
*so begins the life of the child,*
*carried by the birthing waters,*
*from eternity to life.*

On the waters floated Noah's ark,
    a little cosmos in a vast sea
    defined and contained in its sealed box.
    In these waters you have grown, suspended,
    another universe being prepared.

Floating on water came Moses,
    rebirth from the waters.
Into the waters went Israel,
    rebirth through the waters.
Passages in water,
passages upon water,
passages through water,
reaching to the land of life.

The waters within the woman
    are the waters within the earth,
    the primordial waters present at creation.

The waters of birth
    are the Red Sea of deliverance
    through which Israel and each baby pass to be born.

The waters within the womb
    are the still waters of Siloam
    flowing in Zion.
    Trustworthy waters,
    alive with the presence of God.

The waters of birth are the living waters,
    life-giving waters that succor and nourish.
Upon the waters hovers the Spirit.
So begins the life of the world.

# At a Cesarean

Despite preparations and intentions, sometimes a woman cannot give birth without medical intervention. Her cervix cannot dilate sufficiently, her pelvis is narrow, the baby's head is too large, the baby is in distress. Whatever the reason, a cesarean section may have to be performed. Many women are disappointed, fearing that technology has deprived them of a sacred birth. The cesarean section is no less sacred than a vaginal birth, however, and the divine Presence is as present in the hands of the surgeon as in the birth canal of the mother. The power of God resides in human hands and human minds.

## YES BY THE AID OF AN AGENT

*We see Your light:*
    *splendor, radiance,*
    *symbol of divinity,*
*life-giving sun that warms and nourishes,*
*moonrock glowing with reflected power.*
*"We praise You, the creator of lights"*
*and when it is dark, we light our fire.*

*As we light our fire we are creators of fire—*
*creators like You, agents and partners.*
*And we praise You, O creator of lights,*
    *for the lights we do not light*
    *and for the lights we light as the image we are*
    *of You.*

*We taste Your food,*
*we eat the bread.*

*"We praise You who brings forth the bread from the earth."*
*Is the wheat bread?*
*When starving children of famine lands*
  *pick up fallen wheat berries*
  *and put them in their mouths—*
*they will stay starving.*
*We cannot eat the growing wheat,*
*not after we have cultivated the plant to grow more grain,*
*not even after we separate the wheat from the chaff.*
*The wheat can nourish us only once we have cooked, or cracked,*
  *or ground it.*
*But we praise You, provider of bread,*
  *for the wheat that comes forth from the earth*
  *and for the bread that You make from it*
*through us.*

*Some things,*
*we are taught,*
*You do only alone:*
*You brought Israel forth from the Land of Egypt*
  *"not by means of an angel,*
  *not by means of a Seraph,*
  *not by means of an agent."*
*You provide rain for Israel.*
  *"not by an angel*
  *and not by means of an agent."*

*In all other matters You have Your workers,*
*"Moses received Torah from Sinai*
  *not from the mouth of an angel*
  *and not from the mouth of a Seraph*
  *but from the mouth of the King of king over kings,*
  *the Holy Blessed One."*
*But we, the people, received them from Moses,*

God's mediator, God's agent.
No child is created
without a man and a woman.
God, a man, and a woman,
three partners in the birth
and sometimes also:
> wise women
> doctors
> nurses
> midwives
> angels
> Seraphs
> and agents.

There is much to be done
to create a person.

# 10. BIRTH

## Deliverance

Birth is release: release of the mother from the struggles to give birth; release of the child from the dark, now-constricting womb. A child needs space, air, and light. It strains to come out, and the mother labors to free it. The mother releases the child as a liberator releases slaves, as a redeemer releases prisoners. Language encodes the similarity: in English, the liberator and the mother "deliver"; in Hebrew, they both *himlit*.

Bela Yudita's prayer book turns to Psalm 102, where the psalmist speaks about how God looks down from heaven "to hear the groans of the prisoner, to release those condemned to death." It turns this apposite verse into a *segula*, a mystical sentence to be recited during labor and childbirth in the belief that it might afford some magical or mystical help for successful birth. To increase its magical efficacy, the pregnant woman is to recite the verse three times backward and forward from the seventh month on: *"to hear the groans of the prisoner, to release those condemned to death. To death, those condemned, to release, prisoner, groans to hear."*

The mother now wishes to deliver and may ask God to open the womb. The mother who wished and prayed to keep the developing baby safe inside her, now wishes to deliver the child from her womb:

*I would deliver my child,*
*as a prisoner is delivered from his prison,*
*as Israel was delivered from Egypt,*
*as we all would be delivered from our sorrows,*
*as we all would be delivered from Evil.*

*Today I am the deliverer.*
*But I cannot deliver alone.*
*Nor can anyone here deliver for me.*
*I turn to my Deliverer,*
*to the one who delivers us all.*

*I feel the Power in my innermost being*
*as I work to push out my child,*
*to expel that which is part of me*
*and create a separate being.*

*Today the Power of delivery*
*works through me,*
*works with me,*
*to deliver my child.*
*I feel the power that moves mountains,*
*creates liberations,*
*upsets history,*
*brings light to us all.*
*My womb squeezes to move with that Power,*
*to once again loose that Power in the world.*
*I try to channel the infinite Power*
*and so deliver my child.*

Once the child is developed, the child *must* come out. Otherwise, it will die. Like a prisoner, it must be released; it must come out to see the light. A Middle Assyrian text contains a direct prayer for the release of the child: the "sealed-up one":

> Let the one which is sealed up be released.
> Let the being come out
> as an independent being.
> Let it come out quickly
> so that it may see the light of the sun.
> Bring forth that sealed-up one,
> the creation of the gods,
> the creation of humanity.
> Let it come out to see the light.

The delivery of a child is a bringing-forth, a mini-reenactment of the Exodus from Egypt. A verse from the account of the Exodus from Egypt has often been used by Jews as a *segula*. In Exodus, chapter 11, Moses informs Pharaoh of the terrible tenth plague, the killing of the Egyptian first born. Then, predicts Moses, *"All these your servants will come down to me and bow down to me, saying, 'Go out, you and all the people at your feet' and after that I will go out"* and he went out from Pharaoh in anger" (Exod. 11:8). This verse is significant for birth up until after the words "and after that I will go out." On birth amulets it is written with the first letters of each Hebrew word, most frequently only the abbreviation of "go out and all the people at your feet": *ṣ'w h'b (ṣsé 'ata wekhal ha'am asher beraglekha)*. To make this formula even more appropriate, the acronym of the first three words ("Go out, you and all") itself spells out the Hebrew word *tse'u*, "go out." Bela Yudita's prayer book has the woman in the last stages of pregnancy and during labor recite the verse orally. Once again, the magical aura is increased by reciting first forward and then backward, and by repeating the sequence three times. The mystical power of this procedure verse is increased by the fact that the verse has the word "go out" three times. Three times forward and backward yields eighteen times, a particularly appropriate number since 18 is the numerical value of the word "life" and is often used by Jews as a propitious number.

Like the deliverance from Egypt, birth delivery releases a new servant of and partner to God. Moreover, they both involve emergence from straits to wideness. The Hebrew word for Egypt is *Mitsrayim*, which sounds much like a Hebrew word for distress, *metsarim*. But this word, and probably the name for Egypt also, come from the word *tsar*, "narrow". Egypt was two narrow strips of land along the Nile; distress is a tight spot (as in the English "straits"). Narrow was the passageway through the Red Sea. And narrow is the birth canal that stretches to allow the child out.

The delivery of the child also brings a passage from non-life to life. As such, birth is the ultimate model for rebirth, for resurrection and birth after death. The baby is shut in the womb as Lazarus in the tomb, and if not released, will be lost from this world. Jesus' deliverance of Lazarus from the tomb has served Christianity as the great paradigm for bringing someone into life. The most common verse used as a Christian *segula* in amulets and charms is John 11:43, "In the name of the Father and the Son, Lazarus, come forth," sometimes found in a more extended form: *"The Lord, seeing the sisters of Lazarus weeping at his tomb, wept in the presence of the Jews and exclaimed, 'Lazarus, come forth' . . ."*

The mother consciously tries to will the baby out. The womb pushes and contracts to expel the baby. We cannot know whether the baby is also trying to push its way out, or is confused and passive as it feels itself buffeted by a mighty force. For eons people have called upon the child to assist in the process, reminding the baby of the Exodus, of Lazarus, and of other births to encourage it to come forth out of its mother's womb.

## COME FORTH!

*Through the ages we have called you, come!*
*In ancient Babylon, they spoke to you,*
*newest person,*
*still in your mother's womb:*

> *"The way is open for you,*
> *the way is clear . . .*
> *As a desired child,*
> *bring yourself forth."*

*Christians have called to you through the ages:*
*invoking the memory of famous mothers:*
> *Ann bore Mary,*
> *Elizabeth bore John,*
> *Mary bore Jesus.*
> *Come forth, come forth!*

*They invoked the aid of great intercessors:*
*God and Mary,*
*Margaret and Girard.*
*They called upon the saints and the angels.*
*They called you in the name of their savior,*
*they adjured you*
*in the name of Father, Son, and Holy Spirit:*
> *Come forth, come forth!*

*They recalled a great delivery of the past:*
"Jesus said to Lazarus, 'come forth'
and Lazarus came forth."
*As Lazarus came from death to being,*
*so must the baby: come forth!*

*They swallowed their prayers, written on leaves,*
*They wrote them on wax bound on the mother's foot,*
*tied them above the knee.*
*They placed their prayers upon the mother's abdomen*
*calling for the child to be born:*
        *come forth, come forth!*

*Come forth! Come forth!*
*I charge you!*
*Male or female, come forth!*

*Jews have called through the ages,*
*invoking God and Mother Rachel,*
*calling the help of the angels.*

*They recall their great deliverance from Egypt*
        "Go out—you and all the people at your feet"
        ts'u ha-av ts'u ha-av!
        *Come out, come out!*

*Come out, Come out,*
*says the great and awesome prayer,*
puq, pqu, puq.
*Come out, come out!*

*Throughout the ages we have called you*
*and invoked our God for you:*

*And once again, we call to you:*
*Come forth! Come out! Come out!*

# The Voice of the Child

We image a baby able to hear our calls and respond; we visualize a baby born and well; we image a baby praying for its birth, and we hear the voice of the child:

### IN STRAITS

*Narrow, narrow is the path!*
*You deliver us from narrowness.*

*From Mitsraim—Egypt—you brought us forth,*
*In Metsarim—straits—we call upon You.*
    *You answer us expansively.*           (Ps. 118:3)

*Narrow was the path between the waters of the Red*
    *Sea*
*A canyon between two high walls.*
*Then out into the light and bright and wide*
*of the world beyond Egypt.*

*My way is narrow.*
*In the straits I call upon you:*
*Widen my path,*
*deliver me to the light*
*of life.*

## OPEN THE GATES

*Open the gates of righteousness,*
*open the gates of life!*


*I have journeyed in darkness,*
*have floated in the waters I breathed.*
*I have felt the rhythm*
*of the body that sustained me,*
*I have grown.*
*I am ready to see the light,*
*to hear the sounds of the living.*
>        *to taste*
>        *to touch*
>        *to smell.*
>        *to fill my lungs with the air of the world.*


*Now I must leave.*
*The cord of life that binds me to my mother*
>        *will become the bond of death.*          (Ps. 116:3)
*The waters of life that cushion and provide for me*
>        *will turn into streams of destruction.*


*I call your name, O Lord,*
>        *Deliver me!*                             (Ps. 116:4)
>        *Bring me to life!*
>        *Undo the cords that bind me!*            (Ps. 116:16)
*My trust is in you.*                             (Ps. 116:10)
*I will walk before the Lord*
*in the lands of the living.*                     (Ps. 116:9)


*The lord is my strength and might.*

You are my deliverance.     (Ps. 118:14)
I call upon Your right hand, whose mighty deeds
are known.     (Ps. 118:15–16)

    Let me not die, let me live!
    And I will declare the works of God.     (Ps. 118:17)

Open the gates of righteousness.
I will pass through them and praise the Lord.
Here is the divine gate
    through which the righteous enter.     (Ps. 118:19–20)
Today is the day the Lord has made!
This is God's marvelous deed!     (Ps. 118:23–24)
I exult and rejoice.
I enter the world in the name of the Lord.
So may I be blessed.     (Ps. 118:26)

You are my God and I will praise you.     (Ps. 118:28)
With my first breath I call a mighty cry.
    A cry of joy.
    A cry of praise.
    A cry of Presence.
Hail!
and
Hallelujah!

# The Blood of Birth

Birth is accompanied by blood, lots of blood. Whether a vaginal birth or a cesarean section, there is blood. The mother is bloody, the child is covered with blood. Blood is the mark of life, the sign of human existence, and the sight of the blood reminds us of the agreement in our bodies to serve as God's partners in the world.

*In the blood of the mother you come,*
*blood washing over you,*
*purifying you,*
*cleansing you,*
*anointing you—*
*tabernacle of God—*
*at the moment of your consecration.*

*In the blood of life you come,*
*essence of life,*
*purest of the pure.*
*The flowing of blood carries us between worlds.*
*The blood on the child*
*is the blood of the mother.*
*The mother's blood flows; you come to our land of life.*
*Her blood stops flowing; she will stay with you here.*
*Only an instant separates life from death,*
*only a breath and the flow of blood.*

*O my child, you are marked with the substance of life itself.*
*Blood of the covenant,*
*which bonds us to God;*
*blood of the lamb,*
*the blood of delivery.*

*Blood of redemption,*
*blood of life.*

*O Child, my blood of life surrounds you,*
bedamay hayee: *through my blood, may you live.*
*Today your blood of life flows through your own body,*
bedamayikh hayee, bedamayikh hayee,
*through your blood, live!*
*With your blood, live!*

# EPILOGUE

Once the baby is born, the family, the community, and society at large come to recognize and absorb the new child with afterbirth rituals like baptism, circumcision, and naming. At birth, the mother and child become two, and the long, ongoing process of individuation and separation begins. The mother herself may be greeted with celebration, seclusion, or rituals of thanksgiving and reabsorption. But before all this, it is time to pause for a moment, as did Eve, and reflect on what has happened: "For I, with God, have created a human." It is time to give thanks and glory to God and also to give glory to the joy of being a woman and the magnitude of this act of creation, and of the covenantal partnership that produced it.

## THE COVENANT OF CREATION

*In my womb You formed the child,*                    (Ps. 139:13)
    *in my womb, I nourished it.*                   (Ps. 139:16)
*You formed and numbered the baby's limbs,*
    *I contained and protected them.*

*You who could see the child in my depths,*    (Ps. 139:15)
    *I who felt the kicks and the turns,*
*together we counted the months.*

    *Together we planned the future.*
*Flesh of my Flesh,*    (Jer. 1:5; Isa. 49:5)

*form of Your form.*    (Gen. 1:26)
*Another human being upon the earth,*
*a home for God in this, our world.*

# NOTES

Participatory childbirth methods: It would take too much space here to enumerate even the major works about childbirth. This is a very abbreviated bibliography:

## The History of Childbirth

Ann Oakley, *The Captured Womb: A History of the Medical Care of Pregnant Women* (Oxford: Basil Blackworth, 1984) and R. Wertz and D. Wertz, *Lying In: A History of Childbirth in America* (Boston: Beacon, 1978).

## Cultural Analyses

Suzanne Arms, *Immaculate Deception: A New Look at Women and Childbirth in America* (Boston: Houghton Miflin, 1975) and Emily Martin, *The Woman in the Body: A Cultural Analysis of Reproduction* (Boston: Beacon, 1992).

## Psychology of Childbirth

Myra Leifer, *Psychological Effects of Motherhood: A Study of First Pregnancy* (New York: Praeger, 1980) and, most recently, Libby Lee Coleman and Arthur Coleman, *Pregnancy: The Psychological Experience*, revised and expanded edition (New York: Noonday, 1990).

## Philosophy of Reproduction

Mary O'Brien, *The Politics of Reproduction* (New York: Routledge & Kegan Paul, 1983).

## Techniques of participatory childbirth

Constance A. Bean, *Methods of Childbirth* (New York: Quill, 1990).

## Holistic Birth and Medicine

Penny Armstrong, *Bringing Together the Best of Natural Childbirth with Modern Medicine* (New York: Morrow, 1990) and especially Gayle Peterson and Lewis Mehl, *Pregnancy as Healing: A Holistic Philosophy for Prenatal Care*, 2 vols. (Berkeley: Mindbody Press, 1984), with extensive bibliography.

## Detailed Bibliographies

Karen L. Michaelson et al. *Childbirth in America: Anthropological Perspectives* (South Hadley, Mass.: Borgin and Garvey, 1988).

*Mount Zion.* The term *Mount Zion* is not used today for the temple mount, but for a different mountain in the city. In Biblical times, the use is as I described it. On this point see Jon Levenson, *Sinai and Zion* (Minneapolis: Winston Press, 1985).

*Babylonian Incantation* This is text YBC 4603, published by J.J. van Dijk, "une incantation accompagnant la naissance de l'homme" Orientalia 42 (1973) pp 502–507. The translation is my own.

1. X there is a broken word on the tablet here

1.XX there is another broken word here

# QUEST

*Prayers and intercessors*

*Rachel:* For this practice, see Susan Sered, "Rachel's Tomb and the Milk Grotto of the Virgin Mary: Two Women's Shrines in Bethlehem", *Journal of Feminist Studies in Religion* 2 (1986): 7–22.

*Mother's Manual:* Published by A. Frances Coomes, S.J., *Mother's Manual* (Brooklyn: William Hirten, 1973, 1984).

*St. Girard:* This worship is discussed by Marion Bowman, "Devotion to St. Gerard Majella in Newfoundland: The Saint System in Operation and Transition," M.A. thesis, Memorial University of Newfoundland, Department of Folklore, 1985. My thanks to Leonard Primiano for calling my attention to this thesis

## "The Prayer of Hannah"

See BT *Berakhot* 31b, *Pesikta Rabbati* 43, and the late midrashic compendium *Midrash Hagadol* 1:435.

*I will seclude myself.* Alas, this clever plot cannot be the reason that she got pregnant, for as Rabbi Akiva remarks, "If that were so, all barren women could go and shut themselves in with someone and whoever did not misbehave would get pregnant."

### Prayers for Conception

*"Prayer after Immersion"*: This prayer is translated from an unpublished manuscript, JTS MS 4790, found in the rare-book room of the Jewish Theological Seminary library. For more on these prayer books, see below, 236–237.

Belief in the importance of proper thought during intercourse is recorded at length in *Iggeret Haqodesh (The Holy Letter)*, a marriage manual from the thirteenth century probably written by Gillikian. For an edition and English translation see Seymour J. Cohen: *The Holy Letter: A Study in Medieval Jewish Sexual Morality* (Ktav: 1976). This belief also underlies Nachmanides' prayer for the night of intercourse, also from the thirteenth century, in which he prays first for potency and then for the proper conditions to have offspring.

*Tekhine "O Great God"*: The text is presented and translated in *The Merit of Our Mothers: A Bilingual Anthology of Jewish Women's Prayers*, compiled by Tracy Guren Klirs and translated by Klirs, Ida Cohen Selavan, and Gella Schweid Fishman (Cincinnati: Hebrew Union College Press, 1992), 112–33. It is cited from a collection called *Rokhl Weeps for Her Children* (Vilna: 1910). The translation here is my own.

Line 5, *Miriam's well*: For the legend of Miriam's well, see *Mishna Avot* 5:6 and Louis Ginzberg, *Legends of the Jews* 7, 316.

Line 6, *child*: The original has "son," but it is better not to perpetuate this bias in favor of sons. In the Hebrew prayer above, the word *son* is also the generic world for child. Given the culture of the time, in which women were not given advanced educations, the prayer for a "scholar" indicates a desire for a male-child.

*Cosmic union*: In the contemporary scientific image of egg and sperm, the egg has filaments that reach and stick to the sperm. This has replaced the old idea of the passive egg waiting for the fastest sperm to reach it. See Emily Martin, "The Egg and the Sperm," *Signs: Journal of Women in Culture and Society* 16 (1991), 486–501 with the scientific literature cited there.

### To Open the Lock

In ancient Egyptian key amulets, the key was in the hand of Egyptian gods, most often, Khnem. See Robert K. Ritner, "A Uterine Amulet in the Oriental Institute Collection," Journal of Near Eastern Studies, 43 (1984), 209–221. For further studies of the key, see A. Delatte, "Études sur la magie grecque, 4., Amulettes inédites des musées d'Athènes, 14. La Clef de la matrice," Le Musée Belge 18 (1914), 77; A. A. Barb, "Diva Matrix," *Journal of the Warbourg and Courtauld Institute* 16 (1953), 193–238.

The Talmudic passage of the key in the hand of God is found in *BT Ta'anit* 2a *mandrakes:*

The mandrake root looks like a human, and mandrakes are a common charm for fertility. Mandrakes that Leah's son Reuben found marked the end of Rachel's barrenness. The biblical text allows us to decide whether it was the fertility powers of the mandrake that helped Rachel conceive Joseph or the ending of her rivalry with her sister.

*The spell of some long-ago wizard:* The story of Mar Cyprian, who stopped up the wombs of women, is mentioned in an ancient Syriac incantation. Herman Gollancz, *The Book of Protection: Being a Collection of Charms* (London: Henry Frowde, 1912), Codex A, no. 45, li

# FORMATION

Beginning III
*"The Three Partners":* The passage is from *BT Niddah* 31a

Woman Weaving

*From nature to culture:* See Sherry Ortner, "Is Female to Male as Nature is to Culture?" in *Women in Culture and Society,* ed. M. Rosaldo and R. Lamphere (Stanford: Stanford University Press, 1974) and Tikva Frymer-Kensky, *In the Wake of the Goddesses* (New York: Free Press, 1992), 32–44.

*Gender symbols:* These are found in J.J. Van Dijk, "Une Variante du thème de 'l'ésclave de la lune," *Orientalia* 41, (1972), 339–48. See also Harry Hofner, "Symbols for Masculinity and Femininity: Their Use in Ancient Near Eastern Sympathetic Magic Rituals," *JBL* 85 (1964), 326–35.

*Uttu and the creation of clothes:* See the Sumerian myth of Lahar and Ashnan, Bendt Alster and Herman Vanstiphout, eds., "Lahar and Ašnan," *Acta Sumerologica* 9 (1987), 1–43.

*Smamit and Sideros:* The legend of Smamit and Sideros is found on a sixth-to-seventh-century amulet and two magic bowls (amulet 15 and bowls 12a and 12b) published by Naveh and Shaked, *Amulets and Magic Bowls* (Jerusalem: Magnes Press, 1987). The story is told below on p. 110–111.

*Tsitsinako:* For the legends of Tsitsinako see Marta Weigle, *Spiders and Spinsters: Women and Mythology* (Albuquerque: University of New Mexico Press, 1982) and Marta Weigle, *Creation and Procreation: Feminist Reflections on Mythologies of Cosmogony and Parturition* (Philadelphia: University of Pennsylvania Press, 1989), 19–37.

*"Into the hands of a girl child":* Quoted from the texts brought by J.J. van Dijk, op. cit., 346–47.

*A Fantasy of Creation*

Part of this fantasy can be found in *Midrash Tanhuma*, but here I abridge and translate the independent midrashic text, which is printed in *Otsar Hamidrashim.*

*The Ground of Being*

"with men . . . the tillers": An example would be Rib Addi, the king of the city of Byblos around 1500 C.E., who writes, "My field is like a wife without a husband because it is without a tiller." (Amarna letter, *EA* 74:17). See also Carol Delaney, "Seeds of Honor, Fields of Shame" in *Honor and Shame and the Unity of the Mediterranean*, ed. David Gilmore, American Anthropological Association, 35–49.

The Talmudic passage is from *BT Ta'anit* 8a.

The Sumerian pickaxe text is discussed in Tikva Frymer-Kensky, "The Planting of Man: A Study in Biblical Imagery" in *Love and Death in the Ancient Near East: Essays in Honor of Marvin H. Pope*. ed. John H. Marks and Robert N. Good (Guilford, Conn.: Four Quarters Publishing Company, 1987), 131–32 and the literature cited there.

*women are not the ground:* The phrase is from a responsum of Rabbi Yehudah L. Perilimin of Minsk, who says that while a woman is said to be "the ground of the world," she differs from "mother earth" in that she need not nurture the seed implanted in her against her will, that she may "uproot" seed illegally sown. *Responsum Or. Gadol,* no. 31 (1891), cited by David M. Feldman, *Birth Control in Jewish Law* (New York: New York University Press, 1968), 287.

*"Who will plow my vulva":* These lines, spoken by the goddess Inanna, are from "The Herder Wedding Text", analyzed and translated by Thorkild Jacobsen, in *The Treasures of Darkness: A History of Mesopotamian Religion* (New Haven: Yale University Press, 1976), 33–47. The text, Ni 9602, is published by Samuel Noah Kramer, *PAPS* 107 (1963), 505–8.

*Assent*

Mary O'Brien, in her fascinating study *The Politics of Reproduction* (New York: Routledge and Kegan Paul, 1983), details some of the difference that what she calls "the Age of Contraception" has brought in childbirth. Evidence of Talmudic contraception and of infanticide in classical antiquity shows, however, that the age of choice has been with us for some time.

*"The Matriarch Prayer"*

The Italian prayer books are handwritten in Hebrew with occasional instructions in Italian. The first to be published was made for Bela Yudita Kutscher by her husband and was published by Nina Cardin, *Out of the Depths I Call to You: A Book of Prayers for the Married Jewish Woman* (Aronson, 1992). Paula Feldstein has prepared a critical edition of the pregnancy prayers in the

Italian manuscripts found in the Libraries of the Jewish Theological Seminary and the Hebrew Union College, *Eighteenth Century Italian Women's Prayer Books*, Rabbinic thesis for Hebrew Union College-Jewish Institute of Religion, New York, 1993. "The Matriarch Prayer" is the first part of Feldstein's Prayer no. 2 (29–35).

"*Blessing of an Expectant Mother*": This contemporary version is presented in A. Francis Coomes, S. J., *A Mother's Manual* (New York: William Hirten Co, 1973, 1984), 122–25. An early version as presented in the pamphlet *Sanctifying Pregnancy*, published by The Liturgical Press in 1954. Place suggests that parish women's organizations should undertake to acquaint more women with it, and that they might arrange to have it administered following evening services, preferably on or near a feast commemorating Mary's maternity, and that women could then think about it often during pregnancy. Coomes also notes how rarely this blessing is sought and suggests that it be received either at home or at the church.

## "Counting the Days"

I count the forty days from the eighteenth day after fertilization, when *neurulation* begins, and continuing to the beginning of the fetal period, by which time the major organs have begun to develop but are not yet functioning.

## The circle

The intercession for Miriam is preserved in *Abot de Rabbi Natan*, for which see the translation and edition by Judah Goldin, *The Fathers According to Rabbi Nathan* (New Haven: 1955) 55f, q.v. The demand not to die is in *Deuteronomy Rabbah*, see 11:10.

The stories of Moses, Habakkuk, Honi, and especially the general Pompilius are discussed by Judah Goldin in "On Honi the Circle Maker: A Demanding Prayer," originally published in the *Harvard Theological Review* 66 (1963): 233–37 and reprinted in Judah Goldin, *Studies in Midrash and Related Literature*, ed. Barry Eichler and Jeffrey Tigay (Philadelphia: Jewish Publication Society, 1988), 331–35. Goldin suspects that the story of Pompilius and Antiochus, a historical event, served as the model for the others; however, it is equally likely that Pompilius was following an already-established custom, one also followed by Honi.

The story of Habakkuk's circle is in *Midrash Psalms* 77:1. The story of Honi is told in *Mishnah Taanit* 3:8, *BT Ta'anit* 23a, *JT Ta'anit* 3 66d, and Josephus, *Antiquities* 14,22.

God's drawing of a circle around the sea is recalled in Jeremiah 5:22 and Job 38:8–11.

Holding the Key

Early miscarriages were common in antiquity. Jewish legal texts speak of the tragedy of bringing forth a "sandal"—an undifferentiated mass of flesh. This is probably a fetus in the second month, before the hands and feet have emerged. Other varieties of spontaneous abortion, including those before the full formation of the fetus, are mentioned in the *Mishnah Bekhorot* 8:1.

The bibliography of the key amulets is presented above on p. 234. For further information on such uterine magic, see Jean Jacques Aubert, "Threatened Wombs: Aspects of Ancient Uterine Magic," *Greek, Roman and Byzantine Studies* 50 (1989): 421–49.

I thank Rabbi Steve Sager of Durham, North Carolina, for calling this modern amulet to my attention.

AFFIRMATION

A body grows: Shaddai
The midrash is *Midrash Tanhuma*, tazria 8 and see tsav.

"Shaddai"

This celebration of the human body is not meant to ignore the rare child who is born without arms or to increase the suffering of the child or parents by implying a lesser sanctity. We could use the same symbolic reasoning to assert that even though the full name Shaddai is not found on this child's body, the child is a *shay*, a gift from God.

Rite of Passage

I have been using the provisional text and study book edition of the rite of the catechumen published by the United States Catholic Conference, 1974.

"Covenant of Creation"

An earlier version of this covenant has been published by Tikva Frymer-Kensky, "A Ritual for Affirming and Accepting Pregnancy," *Daughters of the King*, ed. Rivka Haut and Susan Grossman (Jewish Publication Society, 1992). This earlier publication includes Hebrew.

The rabbinic passages about being a partner in creation are *BT Shabbat* 110b (by sanctifying Friday night) and *BT Shabbat* 10a (by righteous judgment). Becoming partner in sexual action is from *Iggeret Haqodesh*, chapter 2. For the English text, see Seymor J. Cohen, *The Holy Letter: A Study in Medieval Jewish Sexual Morality* (Ktav, 1976), 60.

"Be fruitful and multiply": Technically, the Jewish Halakhic tradition has held that only the male is obligated by the commandment of "be fruitful and multiply." The reasons for this distinction are explained by Judith Hauptman,

"Maternal Dissent: Women and Procreation in the Mishna," *Tikkun* (1991): 81f. This is a Halakhic issue, and it is clear that by this ritual, in accepting the pregnancy, the woman is obligating herself to this commandment and should, by Halakhic reasoning, therefore be considered fully obligated.

*"I have created a man with the Lord:"* Older translations of Genesis 4:1 say, "I have gotten a man from the Lord," but the biblical verb *qny* means "to create" and is used in this sense for the creation of heaven and earth (Gen. 14:19) and the creation of human innards (Ps. 139:13).

*A home for God:* See BT *Yebamot* 64a.

*"at peace with self and the world"* comes from the "Shehehyanu Prayer" said in hospitals for the mother of a newborn, found in the rabbis' manual edited by Jules Harlowe, 1965 edition, p. 8.

*"Bilhah and Zilpah":* Women have generally added Rachel and Leah and omitted Bilhah and Zilpah. To do so is to deny them their status as mothers of Israel simply because they were not full wives. It will not suffice to claim that the children of Zilpah and Bilhah were among the lost tribes. People from the north, including the children of Bilhah and Zilpah, fled south at the time of the Assyrian conquest. It is wrong to speak of "ten" lost tribes for another reason: Benjamin was exiled with the Northern Kingdom people, as was much of Judah (see Jer. 31:11). If Bilhah and Zilpah are omitted because their tribes were "lost," then Rachel should also be left out, with only Leah remaining as mother of Israel.

*"safe, alive, healthy, and well":* This line is from the *Mi Sheberach* for a woman who has given birth.

*"Torah, love, and righteous acts":* The phrase is from the *Mi Sheberach* used at a naming and at Bar and Bat Mitzvahs. I translate *huppah*, "wedding canopy," as "love" to be as inclusive as possible. The wish can, of course, be modified in any way.

## Loss

We are just beginning to address this silence. See, for a beginning, Merle Feld, "Healing After a Miscarriage," *Response* 14 (1985), reprinted in *Four Centuries of Jewish Women's Spirituality: A Sourcebook,* Ellen Umansky and Dianne Ashton, eds. (Boston: Beacon, 1992), 221; Susan Grossman, "Finding Comfort after a Miscarriage" in *Daughters of the King: Women and the Synagogue.* ed. Susan Grossman and Rivka Haut (Jewish Publication Society, 1992), 284–90; Margaret Gibson, "Country Woman Elegy," Kathleen Frase, "Flowers," and Alta, "104" in *Cries of the Spirit: A Celebration of Women's Spirtuality,* ed. Marilyn Sewell (Boston: Beacon, 1991) 105–7.

*"worlds . . . created and destroyed":* See the *Midrash Bereshit Rabbah* 3, 7; 9,2

*"Has Your right arm withered?":* This section is based on Psalm 77: 9–13. This psalm was written at a time of catastrophe and contains the agony of the psalmist and the determination to continue in faith.

## MIDPASSAGE

### Myth Mothers

*Eve:* See Tikva Frymer-Kensky, *In the Wake of the Goddesses* (New York: Macmillan, 1992) 108–17 and J.A. Phillips, *Eve: the History of an Idea* (San Francisco: Harper and Row, 1984).

### Mothers Divine

The classic studies of the paleolithic goddess are Robert Graves, *The White Goddess.* First American edition New York: Ferrar, Straus & Giroux, 1966. Erich Neumann, *The Great Mother,* Ralph Manheim, tr. (Princeton: Princeton University Press, 1955); E. O. James, *The Cult of the Mother Goddess* (London: Thames and Hudson, 1959); and Maria Gimbutas, *The Gods and Goddesses of Old Europe: 7000 to 3500 BC: Myths, Legends and Cult Images* (London: Thames and Hudson, 1974); and *The Language of the Goddess* (San Francisco: Harper and Row, 1989).

God forms the child in the womb: Jeremiah 1:5; Isaiah 44:2, 24; Isaiah 49:5; Psalm 139: 13–6; Job 10;8–11 and 31:15. God supervises and protects it there: Psalm 22:10; Psalm 71:15; Isaiah 46:3–4. God may determine its destiny there: Jeremiah 1:5; Isaiah 49:1. God supervises the birth in Psalm 22:9; Isaiah 66:9; Job 10:18.

### "Behold the Human"

In John 19:5, Pilate said "Behold the human." In the Vulgate the word is *homo,* in the Greek, *ho anthropos* both mean "human" rather than "male." The Greek to Numbers 24:17, "and the man shall arise from Israel," may show a Messianic sense.

*Theotokos:* This is the Greek term for Mary as the mother of God, not only the mother of the human Jesus.

*The image of god:* For humanity as the image, see Genesis 1:21 and *Gen Rabbah* 34:20: whoever doesn't procreate, it is as if diminished the divine image. For humanity as the place for the presence, see *BT Yebamot* 64a. If there are no descendants, upon whom will the Divine Presence rest?

### "Round Is the Belly, Round Is the World"

*"Ouroboros":* this image of a snake with its tail in its mouth is an ancient symbol and is found as the enclosing element on ancient Egyptian amulets as well as in other ancient iconography. The psychological implications of this symbol have been discussed by Erich Neumann, *The Origins and History of Consciousness* (Princeton: Bollingen Series 42, Princeton University Press, 1973) and Erich Neumann, *The Great Mother: An Analysis of the Archetype,* Ralph Manheim, trans. (Princeton: Bollingen Series 47, Princeton University Press, 1974).

*Eggs in the Jewish calendar:* Haman's Egg is a hard-boiled egg in a pastry basket. It is eaten by Sephardic Jews on the holiday of Purim in early spring. At Passover there are two eggs. There is a roasted egg on the Passover plate, designated as a memory of the festival offering in the temple. Moreover, in addition, the first food eaten between the ceremonial foods and the meal proper is a hard-boiled egg that is dipped in salt water. Unlike the ceremonial foods, the eggs have no special blessing, no mention in the Haggadah. This eating of the eggs is clearly a springtime custom that has entered the Passover seder as a folk practice without official entry into the Haggadah.

*"round for the new year":* At the Jewish New Year's festival, Rosh Hashanah, the meal is begun with apples dipped with honey, for a round sweet year, and the festive bread for Rosh Hashanah is a round hallah, again in order to keep the sense of rounding the year and continuing.

*"I give my love a ring":* These two lines are from an old English folk song.

## Jerusalem, Mountains Surround Her:

For each child as the resting place of Shekhinah, see *BT Yebamot* 63b, 64a and cf. *Gen Rabbah* 34, 20.

## Mandalas

For creating mandalas see Suzanne Fincher, *Creating Mandalas for Insight, Healing and Self Expression* (Boston: Shambhala, 1991) and Rudiger Dahlke, *Mandalas of the World: A Meditating and Painting Guide* (New York: Sterling, 1992).

## "The Child to Come"

The Italian-Hebrew petition is printed in Cardin, *Out of the Depths I Call to You: A Book of Prayers for the Married Jewish Woman* (Northvale, N.J.: Aronson, 1992) 72–77. "Feldstein's Prayer" no. 2 (29–35) begins with the "matriarch prayer" found here on pp. 42–43, and then continues with the petition.

The Old Yiddish petition is taken from the *Seder Tefilah derekh Yesharah*, prepared and edited by Yehiel Mikhl ben Avraham Epstein (Frankfurt-an-der-Oder, 1703). I am grateful to Chava Weissler for providing me with photocopies of the childbirth materials that she identified in her study of these Yiddish devotional prayers, called *tekhines*. More on these devotional prayers is found in "A Cycle of Jewish Mystical Prayers."

*248 parts:* This is the traditional Jewish counting of the number of parts in the human body.

*medium:* in *BT Berachot* 31b, this moderate quality of the child is given as an explanation of the expression "human seed" in Hannah's prayer.

## DANGER AND DREAD

*The childsnatcher:* For Lamashtu as the Pashittu, "snatcher," see von Soden, *Akkadisches Handwörterbuch II* (Harrassowitz, 1972), 845 *pašittu(m)* and the texts cited there.

For a good introduction to Lamashtu, see Walter Farber, "Lamashtu" in *Realexikon der Assyriologie 6* (Berlin, 1983), 439–46; Farber, *Schlaf, Kindchen, Schlaf: Mesopotamische Baby-Beschwörungen und—Rituale* (Winona Lake, Indiana: Eisenbrauns, 1989); and F.A.M. Wiggerman, "Lamaštu, dochter van Anu" in M. Stol, *Zwangerschap en geboorte bij de Babyloniers en in de Bijbel. Met een hoofstuk van F.A.M. Wiggermann* (Leiden: 1983), 95–116.

*"Lamashtu, daughter of An":*

This is my translation of the composite text that can be assembled from the score set out by Walter Farber in his as-yet unpublished edition of the Lamaštu series of incantations. In this series, this is the tenth incantation; the lines are Lam tablet 2, 126f. This particular short incantation is often found on little amulets that may have been worn.

Line 2. *the heroine of the mistresses:* The language here is laconic. The text may be invoking Inanna against Lamaštu. On the other hand, since Inanna is also the daughter of An, also leonine, also a rover, she has much in common with Lamaštu, and indeed, Lamaštu may be the demonic aspect of the fierce Inanna/Ishtar.

Line 4. *alu-demon of humanity:* Is Inanna/Lamaštu the one who fetters the dangerous assaku and the alu demon who belongs to humanity, or who attacks humankind? Again, the language is cryptic.

Line 5. *person:* Even though lú is normally a man, the birth incantations clearly call the parturient woman "the sick man." Clearly, the term is inclusive in medical contexts.

*"Lamashtu"*

This is Lamaštu incantation no. 11, a composite text that I base on the score by Walter Farber. (*Lamaštu 2: 133–47*)

> ÉN DUMU.MÍ *da-nim šá AN-e a-na-[ku]*
> su-ta-a-ku ni-gi-ṣa-a-ku na-mu-ra-a-ku
> É er-ru-ub É us-ṣi
> bi-la-a-ni DUMU.MEš-ki-na lu-š[e-niq]
> a-na KA DUMU.MÍ.MEš-ki-na tu-la-a/UBUR lu-uš-tak-kan
> iš-mi-ma *da-num i-bak-k[i]*
> šá *da-ru-ru dbe-let-DINGIR.MEš il-la-ka di-ma-a-šá*
> am-mi-ni šá ni-ib-nu-ú nu-hal-laq
> ù šá nu-šab-šab-šu-ú ub-bal šá-a-ru
> li-qé-ši-ma a-na tam-tim ZUM šá KUR-i (subartu šá šedi?)

*it-ti GIŠ.ŠINIG a-hi-i u ku-šá-ri a-hi-ii ru-kus-su-ma*
*ki-ma LÚ-UG₆ la i-šú-u ba-la-tu*
*ù ᵈkù-bu la i-ni-qu ši-zib AMA-šú*
*DUMU.MÍ ᵈa-nim ki-na qut-ri ana AN-e È-ma (=E₁₁)*
*la i-na-ahi-is TU₆.ÉN*

*The Lamashtu Series:* This series is being edited by Walter Farber, and I am grateful to him for showing me his manuscript in progress and consulting with me.

### "The Daughter of An"

This is my compilation of three Babylonian incantations.

### "The Testament of Solomon"

In the critical edition by Chester McCown, *The Testament of Solomon* (Leipzig: 1922), the passage is chapter 13 on page 43*. It is often cited as "chapter 57," following Gaster in his classic study of the long history of the childsnatcher incantations, "Two Thousand Years of a Charm against the Child-Stealing Witch," *Folk Lore* 11 (1900): 129–62, reprinted in *Studies and Texts in Folklore, Magic, Medieval Romance, Hebrew Apocrypha and Samaritan Archeology* (London: 1928).

    Another Arabic birth incantation relates how Solomon met the Karina one night and asked her, "Whither are you going," and she replied, "I am going to the one who is in the womb of her mother; I eat its flesh, drink its blood and crush its bones." Solomon then curses her, and she reveals that she has twelve names: whoever hangs them on the wall, she will not approach. These texts have been studied by H. A. Winkler, *Salomo und die Karina. Eine orientalische Legende von der Bezwingug einer Kindbettdämonin durch einen heiligen Helden* (Stuttgart: Veröffentlichungen des Orientalischen Seminars der Universität Tübingen, Abhandlungen zur allgemeiner Religionsgeschichte 4 Heft, 1931). *King Solomon:* King Solomon and the childsnatcher appear frequently in Arabic incantations. In one incantation, he sees an old gray-haired woman with loose hair and claws, and she explains that she is Umm Al-Sibyan, "the mother of children," who comes to women to cause barrenness and miscarriage, and to men to cause sterility. Solomon binds her tightly and will not let her escape until she teaches him the oaths and curses by which people can restrain her.

    *The name amulets: Gaster traces this type of amulet into nineteenth-century Romania. There the charms relate how their protagonist, the archangel Michael, met the demon Avestitza (in oral versions Avezuha), and she gave him nineteen names.*

### Three Against the Childsnatcher

    The amulet and bowls 12a (Jewish National Library Heb 4 6079) and

12b (Metropolitan Museum, N.Y., no., 86.11.259) are published with translation and commentary by Joseph Naveh and Shaul Shaked: *Amulets and Magic Bowls: Aramaic Incantations of Late Antiquity* (Jerusalem: Magnes, 1987), 104–22, 88–197. The amulet corpus is dated archaeologically to the fifth–sixth century C.E., and Naveh and Shaked believed that the story went from Israel to Babylon.

A full Greek manuscript was published by Perdrizet and reprinted in Naveh-Shaked, *Amulets and Magic Bowls*, 112–14, 21. The manuscript ends with the statement that the device will not cause harm to those who use it. Two more Greek versions were published in Leo Allatius, *De templis Graecorum* (1645), 126–29, 133–35), and translated by Gaster. These manuscripts mention their purpose as protective amulets.

A nineteenth-century Romanian manuscript, presented by Gaster, tells a similar story involving Saint Sisoe, Meletia, and the devil. In this text, the devil swears "by the Lord, who created heaven and earth, that wherever he would see the name or the book of the Holy Sisoe he would have no power to harm or to hurt the people."

## Ben Sira's story of Lilith

For the text and details, see Eli Yassif, *The Tales of Ben Sira in the Middle Ages: A Critical Text and Literary Studies*, in Hebrew (Jerusalem: Magnes Press, Hebrew University, 1984). The story told here is from the Italian manuscript tradition of this story; the manuscript tradition from Northern Europe has a somewhat fuller tale. David Stern and Abraham Myrkin have published a translation of the printed version in "Rabbinic Fantasies," *JPS* (1990).

## SSSS

*Swny Swswny Snygly:* the names of the three helpers in the silver amulet from Israel.

*iron-sharp Sideros:* the name of the child killer in the silver amulet. According to Naveh and Shaked, the name should be understood as the Greek word "iron."

*Smamit:* The mother in the Aramaic story preserved on this amulet; the name means "spider."

*"May the one who has measured":* This is the verse that Sideros quoted in his promissory oath not to kill.

*Swny Sswyny Sngrw Weartyqw:* the helpers in the Aramaic incantation bowl.

*Werzelya:* the demon in the Ethiopian amulets; the name is probably the Aramaic word for "iron."

*Sanvai, Sansanvai, Semongolof:* the angel helpers in the Jewish tradition.

*The strangler:* the demoness in late Syria: *emma hanoqta d-talye* ("the mother who is a strangler of children"), Gollancz (1812), 60–65, who is killed by 'abd-išo.

*Al:* for the Al, the Persian childsnatcher. See Wilhelm Eilers, *Die Al: Ein persisches Kindbettgespenst. Bayerische Akademie der Wissenschaften. Philosophisch-historische Klasse* (Munich 1979).

*Sisinious Sines Sinodore:* These are the helpers in the Greek version of the stories. See Perdrizet, 1922 q.v. In Greek tradition they are considered saints, and the attacking power is the demoness Ghyllou; the saints inform her, "We are going to be pursuers in the name of God, and we shall seize her."

*Susneyos:* the name of the helper (the woman's husband) in the Ethiopian amulets published by Worrell, 1909.

*st zt:* See the Arslan Tash inscription discussed by Gaster, "A Canaanite Magical Text," *Orientalia* 11 (42):41–79.

*sator:* For the sator square in childbirth, see Thomas Rogers Forbes, *The Midwife and the Witch* (New Haven: Yale University Press, 1966), 64–79.

*saroer:* the loosening word on Greco-Egyptian uterine amulets.

*Levi-Strauss:* See Claude Lévi-Strauss, *Structural Anthropology* (New York: Basic Books, 1965), chapter X "The Effectiveness of Symbols", 186–205.

*Fear of women:* See Dorothy Dinnerstein, *The Mermaid and the Minotaur: Sexual Arrangement and Human Malaise* (New York: Harper & Row, 1976) and H. R. Hays, *The Dangerous Sex: The Myth of Feminine Evil* (New York: Pocket Books, 1964). For the childsnatcher as the dark mother, see Jacques Bril, *Lilith où la mère obscure* (Paris: Payot, 1981).

Dread:
*Shekhinah* is the immanent Presence of God. "Under the wings of Shekhinah" is a Hebrew phrase.

stone Amulets

These are discussed by Thomas Rogers Forbes, *The Midwife and the Witch* (New Haven: Yale University Press, 1966) 64–79. The Talmudic stone is in *BT Shabbat E.* See *Tosefta Qiddushin* V 17.

For the Aetatis stone, add to Forbes's discussion the discovery of Mesopotamian use by Georges Dossin, "L'Euphrate au secours des parturientes," *AIPHOS* 20 (1968–72), 213–21.

*silver amulets:* The original publication is by G. Barkay, *Ketef Hinnom* (Jerusalem: Israel Museum Catalogue 274, 1986).

The use of the priestly blessing by the Samaritans in Nablus in 1940 is reported by Gaster, "A Canaanite Magical Text," *Or.* 11 (42), 41–79.

SEFER HARAZIM: See M. Margalioth, *Sepher Ha-Razim: A Newly Discovered Book of Magic from the Talmudic Period,* 1966; for the English, see M. A. Morgan, *Sepher Ha-Razim: The Book of Mysteries,* 1983

*Hebrew amulets:* For these see T. Shrire, *Hebrew Magic Amulets: Their Decipherment and Interpretation* (New York: Behrman House, 1966) 152 and plate 22.

*Syriac charm:* Published by Hermann Gollancz, *The Book of Protection: Being a Collection of Charms* (London: Henry Frowde, 1912).

*Anglo-Saxon and Latin charms:* These are collected by Forbes, *The Midwife and the Witch*, op.cit, 80–93.

*St. Margaret Amulets:* Many copies of the story of St. Marguerite in Latin have been found. In addition, the first vernacular translation was made into Anglo-Saxon around 1000. The great French poet Wace is alleged to be the author of a long account of the life of Margaret in French verse(c. 1100). This is edited by Hans Eric Keller, *Wace, La Vie de St. Marguerite*, Beihefte für Romanischen Philologie (Tübingen: Max Niemeyer Verlag, 1990). This French poem was widely distributed and is found in books of hours and prayer rolls from the fifteenth century.

*Injunction against birth incantations:* This and other examples are cited by J. H. Aveling, M.D., *English Midwives: Their History and Prospects* (London: Churchill, 1872), 1–5. Forbes, *The Midwife and the Witch*, discusses the silencing process.

*French birthing bag:* Reported by A. Aymar, "Le Sachet accoucheur et ses mystères," *Annales du Midi* 38(1926):297–303.

## Prayer

*The birth of Rabbi Ishmael:* See the midrash *eleh ezkerah*, in *Ozar hamidrashim* 440–41

*Mother Rachel:* Jeremiah 31:11–21. For an understanding of this passage and of the monotheist urge to find advocates in Heaven, see Frymer-Kensky, *In the Wake of the Goddesses,* 162–67.

"Memorare": This prayer comes from Anthony Buono, *Favorite Prayers to Our Lady* (New York: Catholic Book Publishing Company, 1991), 130. Buono found the prayer in an earlier book, *Prayers for the People of God,* and traced it to an even earlier book, *Mother Love,* published in 1826. The prayer gives all signs of having been written much earlier (personal communication from Anthony Buono).

*The cult of St. Marguerite (Margaret):* Nicholas of Cusa condemned this belief in 1455. See Reames, *The Legenda Aurea,* 50. The Reformers, of course, continued to condemn the use of Margaret tales.

I am indebted to Virginia Reinburg for sharing her chapter on St. Margaret from her as-yet-unpublished book on popular prayer. According to Reinburg, Margaret may not have existed, and the details of her life are typical of the vitae of other saints. The Marguerite prayers are collected in Pierre Rézeau, *Les Prières aux saints en francais à la fin du moyen âge,* vol. 2 (Geneva: Librairie Drox, 1982), 319–35. In an early study, Jolie reports that one manuscript in the Normandy Library, no. 17002, is from the tenth century. See A. Jolie, *La Vie de Sainte Marguerite: Memoires de la société des antequaires de*

*Normandie*, (1880), 10. In his edition of Wace's French translation, Keller reports that Wace used two Latin versions and suggests a date of composition of about 1135 C.E. (Wace, *La Vie de S. Marguerite*).

*"those who remember me"*: translation from the Latin of *La Légende dorée*, by Jacques de Voragine, as quoted by P. Albarel, "L'Oraison de sainte Marguerite pour les femmes en couches," *La Chronique Médicale* 31 (1924):231–33.

Albarel cites the placing of the life on the breast:

> *Tenez: mettez sur vostre pis*
> *La vie qui cy est escrite:*
> *Elle est de saincte Marguerite*
> *Si serés tantost delivrée*

## "A Madame Saincte Marguerite"

This is the version that appears in H. de Lalung, *L'Accouchement à travers les âges et les peuples*. Les Laboratoires "cortial"

> *Madame Saincte Marguerite,*
> *Digne vierge de Dieu eslite,*
> *Qui, pour l'amour-Dieu, nostre Sire,*
> *Souffris tourmens et grief martyre;*
> *Qui à Dieu fis mainte requeste*
> *Quant on te voult couper la teste*
> *Et, par espécial, que femme*
> *Grosse d'enfant qui à toy, Dame,*
> *De cueur dévot retourneroit*
> *Et ton ayde requerroit*
> *Que Dieu de périr la gardast*
> *Et de l'ayder point ne tardast;*
> *Cy te supplie, vierge honorée*
> *Noble Martyre et bien eurée*
> *Que Dieu veuille pour moy prier*
> *Et doulcement Luy supplier*
> *Que par sa pitié Il me conforte*
> *Pour bien oeuvrer livre que je porte.*
> *Sans péril d'âme ne de corps*
> *Fasse cettuy livre yssir hors;*
> *Resjouir moult mires que je le voye*
> *Et puisse-je, toute ma vye,*
> *Toy mercyer pour si grand bienfaict.*
>     *Ainsi il-soict!*

The critical edition is in Pierre Rezeau, *Les Prières aux saintes en français à la fin du moyen âge* (Geneva: Librairie Droz, 1982), text no. 156, who dates it to the fifteenth century. His manuscript has considerable differences.

*Luther's objection:* "*Luther's Works*" 45:38, quoted by Margaret L. Hammer, *Giving Birth: Reclaiming Biblical Metaphor for Pastoral Practice* (Louisville: Westminster/John Knox, 1994), 132.

## "Illustrious St. Marguerite"

Reported by P. Albarel, "L'Oraison de sainte Marguerite, pour les femmes en couches," in *La Chronique médicale*, the book was titled *l'Office de la Vierge Marie suivant la réformation du S. Concile de Trente, Oraison pour invoquer sainte Marguerite, lorsqu'une femme est en travail d'enfant.*

> Illustre sainte Marguerite,
> Dont les vertus e le mérite
> Vous ont procuré dans les cieux
> Un trône des plus glorieux;
> Qui dès votre plus tendre enfance
> Consacrâtes votre innocence
> A l'Epoux de la chasteté,
> Au Dieu de toute pureté;
> Qui, dans le cours de votre vie,
> De mille merveilles remplie,
> Sous votre pied victorieux
> Foulant un dragon furieux
> Sûtes faire expirer sa rage;
> Qui souffrites avec courage
> Les supplices et les fureurs
> De vos cruels persécuteurs;
> Qui, pour prix de votre victoire,
> Régnez au séjour de la gloire,
> Goûtant les délices des Cieux
> Avec les Esprits bienheureux,
> J'implore, ô Vierge tromphante!
> Votre protection puissante,
> Vos mérites, votre crédit,
> Auprès du Sauveur Jésus-Christ.
> Ce divin Sauveur vous accorde,
> Dans sa grande miséricorde,
> Tout ce que vous lui demandez
> Pour les mortels infortunés
> Voyez l'état où je soupire!
> Obtenez-moi, Vierge et Martyre,

*Que le Seigneur, par ses faveurs,*
*Me soulage dans mes douleurs,*
*Qu'il me conserve et me conforte,*
*Avec le fruit que mon sein porte,*
*Pour qu'il naisse au jour destiné,*
*Et qu'aussitôt qu'il sera né,*
*Grâces à sa bonté suprême*
*Il reçoive le saint Baptême.*
*Qu'il vive dans la sainteté*
*Dans le temps et*
      *l'éternité.*

*St. Gerard card:* For others, see the M.A. thesis cited on p. 233.

## A Cycle of Mystical Jewish Prayers

One of the Italian manuscripts has been published by Nina Cardin, *Out of the Depths I Call to You: A Book of Prayers for the Married Jewish Woman* (Aronson, 1992) 72–77. Paula Feldstein has prepared a critical edition of the pregnancy prayers in the manuscripts in the libraries of the Jewish Theological Seminary and the Hebrew Union College-Jewish Institute of Religion in New York City, *Eighteenth-Century Italian Women's Prayer Books*, rabbinic thesis for Hebrew Union College-Jewish Institute of Religion, New York, 1993.

The Yiddish *tekhines* were brought to my attention by Chava Weissler, who gave me photocopies of the appropriate pages of the *Seder Tefilah derekh yesharah*, the *Seder bakashos und Tekhinos* (Fürth, 1762), and the *Seder Tekhinos*. (In my studies I used a 1752 Amsterdam copy of the *Seder Tekhinos* from the JTS library, the photocopy of which was clear. A spot check of copies from the Bodleian copy of the 1650 printing showed that they were virtually identical.

In these translations I have used primarily the *Kitsur Shelah;* the Italian prayer book copied for Bela Yudita Coen and published by Nina Cardin; the unpublished Italian prayer book JTS 4525; a devotional manual, the *Little Book of Musar*, published in 1700; a prayer book, *Seder Tefilah Derekh Yesharah*, edited by Yehiel Mikhl ben Avraham Epstein, Frankfurt an-der-Oder, 1700s; and two compendia of Yiddish *tekhines*, the *Seder Baqashos Utêhînos*, published in Fürth in 1740, and the *Seder Tekhines*, Amsterdam 1650. There are many other exemplars of these prayers, and it is clear that a treasured group of prayers for late pregnancy and childbirth was copied and transmitted both in the learned Hebrew tradition and in the Yiddish of Central and Eastern Europe.

## "Like a Hen"

In the *Seder Baqashos Utehinos*, the two versions are slightly different from each other—enough to show that the Yiddish is not a translation of the Hebrew preserved here but is an independent version of the old prayer. In the *Little Book of Musar*, the woman says it for herself (in Yiddish) during labor.

I translate the prayer here as it occurs in the *Kitsur Shelah*, with the exception that I have included the longer form "as a hen lays an egg" (from the Yiddish version in *Seder Baqashos*) instead of "like a hen," and that I omit references to "my wife." In Feldstein's edition of the Hebrew manuscripts, this is prayer no. 3, pp. 41–44

*"the writ of Eve"*: This writ refers to the statement in Genesis 3:16: "Greatly will I multiply your labor and conception and in travail you will bring forth children." In the Fürth compendium, the Hebrew version, meant to be recited by scholars, quotes the Hebrew verse. The Yiddish does not mention the writ at all and only says, "May she give birth without pain." The *Little Book of Musar* quotes the whole verse in Yiddish. The idea that righteous women are not included in the writ of Eve goes back to the Talmud, BT Sota 12a and cf. Shmot Rabbah 1:23.

*Prayer for well-being*: The Yiddish prayer continues, "And she and her husband should raise it with full heart in God's service, (for Torah and good deeds, for the marriage canopy, for a good life and well-being, wealth, honor and ease). And let her and her child not be bodily harmed, neither in inner parts or outer limbs. And may she and her child be fresh and healthy so that they can serve you. For in you is our hope that you help all who turn to you in truth. (May the words of my mouth and the meditation of my heart be acceptable to you, my rock and my redeemer.) Amen." The phrases in parentheses are in Hebrew.

*Violating the Sabbath*: This rule is already in the Talmud, BT Shabbat 128a–129a. For giving a pregnant woman forbidden foods, see BT Yoma 82a

*Amen*. Bela Yudita's prayerbook combines this with the next prayer and therefore ends this part Amen Selah.

## "Zera Qayyama"

The text translated here is from the Yiddish/Old Yiddish prayer book, *Seder Baqashos Utehinos Tehinos ubbaqashos* (Fürth: 1762).

*Anenu litanics*: For the Anenu litanies, see below, pp. 198–203

*Zera Qayyama*. The Italian prayer books use the phrase *zera shel qayyama* ("a living seed").

*"merciful are Your mercies"*: The Italian prayer books do not have this paragraph, for the prayer has been joined to "Like a Hen." The *Kitsur Shelah* is said in the plural and has "because your mercies are many." Can it be that the phrase "O Merciful One, merciful are your mercies" is consciously aware of using the relationship between the words "merciful, mercies" (*rahum, rahamim*) and "womb" (*rehem*)?

*"the key"*: For this key, see above, pp. 19–21 and 49–51. There are variants. The *Kitsur Shelah* has the most elegant grammar but reads "this key" (*hazzeh*) instead of "birthing" (*hayyah*). At some point in the chain of tradition,

someone no longer understood the word *hayyah*. The Italian prayer book explains the word and simplifies the grammar: "the key of birthing and of giving birth which has not been handed to an angel." Such misunderstandings and variations are clear indications that the source of the prayer is older.

*"straits"*: The verse is from Psalm 118:5. *Straits* is a general word for "distress," but it is particularly appropriate for childbirth, for it means narrowness, in Hebrew and in English. See the poem "in straits," p. 225. The *Kitsur Shelah* adds Psalm 20 immediately at this point, with instructions to read it to the end. Bela Yudita's prayer book does not add anything here but places Psalm 20 immediately after this prayer. For the use of Psalm 20 in childbirth, see pp. 180–181.

*"holy mothers"*: This version of the prayer actually has "our holy fathers." It is often the custom in the Yiddish-speaking world to use the word *fathers* as "ancestors," even when mothers are meant. The other versions all have "our holy mothers."

## "The Judgment Prayer"

In the *Seder Baqashos Utehinos*, the *"Zera Qayyama"* prayer is immediately followed in Yiddish by a version of "The Judgment Prayer." These are to be said from the seventh month on. Similarly, the *Musar Bichel* provides that this prayer should be said daily, during the Amidah, from the seventh month on. The Italian prayer books contain the same prayer in Hebrew with instructions to recite it during labor. The *Seder Baqashos Utehinos* also includes a fuller version of this same prayer, with instructions that when labor pains begin the woman should recite it "with great devotion."

I am translating here the Hebrew text of the unpublished Italian prayer book JTS 4525. In Paula Feldstein's edition, this is prayer no. 17, pp. 59–63. Bela Yudita's prayer book does not have the key phrase "block up every gap in your holy throne," which appears both in this manuscript and in the Yiddish versions.

*A time of judgment*: BT Shabbat 32b.

*Stopping Menashe's prayer*. This is from *Pesikta de Rav Kahana* 24:11: In BT Sanhedrin 103a, Rabbi Yohanan presents a teaching from Rabbi Shimon Bar Yochai: "Why is it written *vayehater lo* (it was dug for him) when it should be *vaye'ater lo* (he was entreated for him)? This is to teach that the Holy Blessed One made a hole in the heavens in order to receive his (Manasseh's) repentence because of (in order to circumvent) the attribute of justice." This seems to be a version of the same story. The connection between *wayehater* and *Waye'ater* is also remarked on in the *Peskita*, which points out that in Aramaic they are pronounced the same. The reference in the Talmud is to 2 Chronicles 33:13, which in our current Masoretic texts is in fact written *waye'ater lo*.

*"What are you doing?"*: The *Musar Bichl* softens this with "what are you

doing, beloved God?" The source is Isaiah 45:9: "Will the clay say to the Former, what are you doing?"

"gap in your holy throne": translated according to the Yiddish. The Hebrew has "in your holy dwelling," which is ambiguous, and the Yiddish accords well with the midrash.

"tears of Hannah": The Musar Bichl adds, "and the tears of all pious women."

"May the words of . . . my heart": This, the final verse of Psalm 19, is a frequent ending to prayers.

## "The Doe and the Fiery Creatures"

In Feldstein's edition, this is prayer no. 6, pp. 54–55. My version is based on both the Italian and Yiddish. It is not meant to be a comprehensive "critical edition" but to indicate the closeness of the Hebrew and Yiddish traditions. The Yiddish prayer from Fürth begins with a striking request to angels Michael, Gabriel, and Akatriel. This prayer is not found in the Hebrew but also begins another Yiddish prayer in the Fürth compendium. It is translated separately with the other intercessor prayers on p. 126.

YETEDOT: It should be noted, however, that yetedot is used in a very suggestive way in one of the High Holiday Piyyutim written about the same time, and still included in the Yom Kippur prayer book. Except for this line, I am translating the Hebrew/Aramaic version.

"my petition": The Hebrew here spells petition shelati instead of She'elati. This is a direct reference to the petition of Hannah and the response to her in 1 Samuel 1:17, in which the word for petition is spelled in just this way.

"May the spirits": This line is read here from the Yiddish. The Hebrew only has "who are called yetedot, pegs."

"the Other Side": the demonic world. The Yiddish here says "Satan."

"serve You and bless Your name": For this paragraph the Yiddish has, "I also beg the blessed name to have good children with God's help who will be great in Torah and good deeds to serve the Holy Blessed One."

"holy living seed": The Yiddish text has the words "kosher human seed" in Hebrew, and then "that they should live for your service" in Yiddish.

"The Lord of Hosts is with us": This concluding sequence consists of the final verses of Psalm 46:12; Psalm 84:13; and Psalm 19:15. Instead of this sequence, Seder Baqashos continues with a prayer that the child be born healthy, that the mother have milk to feed and strength to raise the child, and that there be no injury to mother or children.

### A Month of Anticipation

A ninth-month ritual was created by Shoshana Zondervan when she gathered her friends together on the evening of the new moon in the ninth month. Her ritual calls for friends to come bringing a fruit symbolic of a wish that they make for her and an egg-shaped candle. They symbolically transfer their energy to her by chanting her name, she talks about her pregnancy, and they sing, dance, and eat together. Such a ritual moment provides joy and *communitas*. See Shoshana Zonderman, "Spiritual Preparations for Parenthood," *Response: A Contemporary Jewish Review* 14 (Spring 1985):32.

A seventeenth-century Jewish set of religious teachings provides for a very different ritual: the husband and wife fast and give charity, place their affairs in order, and then pray. The focus here is on invoking God's aid in the dangerous time to come for the woman and the child. The prayer is then said daily thereafter.

### The Counting-up Ritual

Advent calendars are often bought but can also be homemade. Omer calendars have been the occasion for some beautiful Jewish folk art. They, too, can be homemade.

*"no one person must complete it"*: see *Pirkey Avot* 2:16.

### "Thoughts for the Ninth Month"

There are nine months from Sivan to Nisan.

## AWAITING THE HOUR

*When technology conquers nature*: See the works of Robbie Davis-Floyd, "The Technological Model of Birth," *Journal of American Folklore* 1100 (1987):479–96 and "Birth as an American Rite of Passage," in Karen Michaelson et al., *Childbirth in America*.

*Sefer Raziel*: The citation and photo are JTS MS 8115.

### A Modern Wall Plaque

To obtain a copy, contact Betsy Plotkin Teutsch: 629 W. Cliveden St., Philadelphia, PA 19119.

*"The Lord will answer you"*: *Midrash Tehilim* 20:4. As a comment on the same verse, the midrash to Deuteronomy, *Deuteronomy Rabba II*, 11 brings this quote: "The Lord answer you in the day of straits"—"What is the meaning of the day of straits"? Resh Lakish said, "Just as, when a woman in labor is seated in the birthing chair, people say to her, " 'May the one who answered your mother answer you', so said David to Israel, " 'The one who answered Jacob will answer you.' "

## Unbinding

The Lucina prayer is related in Ovid *Fasti* III, 255f. Note also the Roman legend of Lucinda delaying birth as long as she sat outside the birth room with her fingers clasped together.

"*I have done the binding*" is related by Pliny, Natural History, 28, 42 and cited by Ricardus Heim *Incantamenta magica graeca Latina*.

"*rose of Jericho*": For this and other customs, see Jacques Gélis *History of Childbirth*, Rosemary Morris, trans. (Boston: Northeastern University Press, 1992), 117. The French title is, *L'Arbre et le fruit*.

Prayer to Uttu: The text is Theophilus Meek BA 10/1, edited by Borger, "Der Sonnengott als Helfer der Gebärenden," *Orientalia* 54, 14–18.

The key in the Cairo Genizah: The text is

T.-S. NSS 322 10. Now published as Peter Schäter and Shaul Shaked, *Magische Texte aus der Kairoer Genizah*, band I, Tübingen, J. C. B. Mohr (Paul Siebeck) 1994, pp. 83–107.

*Silim-ma*:

The lines are:

> *munus-bi silim-ma ù-tu-ud-da*
> sinniš-tu ši-i šal-meš li-it-tal-lak
>
> *ù-tu-ud-da ti-la šà-bi silim-ma*
> li-lid-ma lib-lut šá hib-bi-šú li-ṣìr
>
> *igi-dingir-zu silim-ma he-en-DU-DU*
> ina ma-har DINGIR-ti-ka šal-meš lit-tal-lak
>
> *silim-ma ù-tu-ud-da ka-tar-zu hé-en-si-il-la*
> šal-meš li-lid-ma dà-li-li-ka lid-lul

## "Enrobing"

*purple*: A good example of the use of ARGAMAN (purple) on amulets is on a silver one shaped like a knife with a three-line inscription on the blade. The first line has the initial letters of Genesis 49:12—"Joseph is a fruitful bough, a fruitful bough by a spring whose branches climb the wall"—and then the acronym ARGAMAN (purple). The second and third lines explain this acronym: Uriel, Raphael, Gabriel, Michael, Nuriel, and then the statement "[Let this amulet be] a protective hedge for the bearer of this amulet, so may it be God's will." On the handle and across the guard are the names of the healing angels Sanvai, Sansanvai, and Semongolof. This amulet has been published by Theodore Schrire in *Hebrew Magic Amulets*.

*linen*: In Leviticus 6, the priest wears linen to put ashes on the altar and then changes clothes to carry them outside. In Leviticus 16, the priest enters the shrine in the sacred linen tunic; after the ritual, he bathes and puts on regular clothes. Ezekiel 42:14 explains that the priests take off their consecrated garments before they leave the holy space; Ezekiel 44:19 makes it clear that this is so that ordinary people will not have contact with them.

In Ezekiel's vision, in Ezekiel 9, a man dressed in linen carries a writing case and puts a mark on the forehead of those who escape destruction. In Daniel's vision (Daniel 10), a man dressed in linen comes to explain and calculate the apocalypse.

*The robe* (Hebrew *me'il*) is so special that it becomes the identifying mark: when Saul is at the necromancer's, he realizes that she has called up the spirit of Samuel when the figure appears wearing a robe.

### For a Speedy Delivery

*Enki and Ninhursag:* Translation by Thorkild Jacobsen, *The Harps that Once: Sumerian Poetry in Translation* (New Haven: Yale University Press, 1987), 191–92.

Asarluhi's Address: The text is Köcher, BAM 248, 4, 2–3, Erich Ebeling, ed., *Archiv für Geschichte der Medizin* 14 (1923):72–73. This translation is from Benjamin R. Foster, *Before the Muses: An Anthology of Akkadian Literature*, vol. 2 (Bethesda: CDI Press 1993), 892.

### "Michael Prayer"

Jewish Theological Seminary manuscript 4625
   *go out:* For the use of this verse in childbirth see pp. 221–222.

### "Reciting Famous Births"

From a magical "recipe" book found in the Cairo Genizah T.-S. NSS 322.10, op. cit., p. 254.

### The Psalms of birth

For the ritual magical usage, see Joshua Trachtenberg, *Jewish Magic and Superstition: A Study in Folk Religion* (New York: Atheneum, 1939), 202.

Psalm 20 is so appropriate for childbirth that in Bela Yudita's Italian prayer book it is to be recited twelve times. Moreover, contrary to the strong Jewish tradition of not changing biblical texts while citing them, when the psalm is recited for childbirth, this prayer book changes the "you" in "the lord will help you" to the feminine form.

## LABOR

*The debate about anesthetics:* In 1847, Simpson wrote *Answer to the Religious Objection against the Employment of Anaesthetic Agents in Midwifery and Surgery*. For discussion and references, see H. J. Zimmels, *Magicians, Theologians and Doctors:*

*Studies in Folk Medicine of the 12–19 Centuries* (London: Goldstein, 1952). The use of painkillers did not present a problem in Jewish thinking, where the operative principal was that the ways of the Torah are pleasant. Proverbs 3:17 and Genesis 3:16 could be interpreted to refer to the sorrows of raising children (cf. Sforno's commentary ad loc., Italy fifteenth century).

*"Prayer of the Pregnant Woman":* The text is quoted by Jacques Gélis in *History of Childbirth*, Rosemary Morris, trans. (Boston: Northeastern University Press, 1992), 155, taken from Godeau, *Instructions et Prières Chrétiennes* (1646). Gélis believes that the prayer was written under Jansenist influence.

*The woman in Revelation:* Revelation 12:1–2

*Bishop Anselm: Prayers and Meditations of St. Anselm with the Proslogion,* translation and introduction by Sr. Benedicta Ward (London: Penguin, 1973), 153, cited by Margaret L. Hammer, *Giving Birth: Reclaiming Biblical Metaphor for Pastoral Practice* (Louisville: Westminster/John Knox, 1994), 105.

*Julian of Norwich:* Julian of Norwich, *Showings*, chapter 60. For a study of this motif, see Caroline Walker Bynum, *Jesus as Mother: Studies in the Spirituality of the High Middle Ages* (Berkeley: University of California Press, 1982).

*Léonie Caldecott:* cited from "Inner Anatomy of a Birth," in Linda Hurcombe, ed., *Sex and God* (New York: Routledge and Kegan Paul, 1987), 147–60.

*Margaret L. Hammer: Giving Birth: Reclaiming Biblical Metaphor for Pastoral Practice* (Louisville: Westminster/John Knox, 1994), 210.

*Holy labor pains:* For Mother Zion, see Micah 4:10. For "birth pangs of the Messiah," see Roger D. Aus, "The Relevance of Isaiah 66:7 to Revelations 12 and 2 Thessalonians 1," *Zeitschrift für das Neutestamentliches Wissenschaft und die Kunde der Alterer Kirche* 37 (1976):252–68. Aus assembles the Apocryphal and rabbinic references. For the laboring God, see Isaiah 42:14.

*The struggle with chaos:* Chaos is usually represented by the turbulent cosmic waters. For Babylonian myth, see the battle of Marduk and Tiamat recorded in *Enuma Elish*. In the Bible the cosmic waters are called variously "sea," "Rahab," "Tanin," and "Leviathan." The bibliography on these passages is vast. Syntheses can be found in Bernhard Andersen, *Creation vs. Chaos: The Reinterpretation of Mythical Symbolism in the Bible* (New York: Association Press, 1967); John Day, *God's Conflict with the Dragon and the Sea,* University of Cambridge Oriental Publications 35 (Cambridge: Cambridge University Press, 1985); and John Levenson, *Creation and the Persistence of Evil* (Princeton: Princeton University Press, 1994).

*Redemptive suffering:* The idea of the "suffering servant" first appears in the Exilic prophet Deutero-Isaiah (Isaiah, chapters 40f). In Isaiah chapter 53, the servant of God suffers in order to redeem the misdeeds of others. In Christianity this became one of the major ways of understanding the Crucifixion. In Judaism, after the Crusades, Isaiah was interpreted to refer to the people of Israel, who were being oppressed and tortured far beyond any possibility of explanation as punishment.

*A positive view of birth pain:* These ideas are presented by Gayle Peterson and Lewis Mehl, *Pregnancy as Healing: A Holistic Philosophy for Prenatal Care*, 2 vols. (Berkeley: Mindbody Press, 1985). Margaret L. Hammer also suggests that it reminds us of our limits. See Hammer, "Birthing: Perspectives for Theology and Ministry," *Word and World* 4 (Fall 1984):391–400 and Hammer, *Giving Birth: Reclaiming Biblical Metaphor for Pastoral Practice* (Louisville: Westminster/John Knox Press, 1994) 160–77.

## "hil kayoleda" Like a Birthing Woman

*("the high mountain of my pain. . . .")*
This is based on Isaiah 40:9–10: "O Zion, bringer of glad tidings, ascend the high mountain, proclaim to the daughters of Judah, 'behold your God.'" For the many parallels between the pregnant woman and Woman Zion, see "Jerusalem, Mountains Surround Her" and "Walk Around Zion" on pp. 90–92 and 158.

*"the battle is on"*: For this image of labor as battle, see the Middle Assyrian medical text published by Lambert, "A Middle Assyrian Medical Text," *Iraq* 31(1969): 32, lines 37–41.

Magical "recipe" book: T.-S. NSS 322.10. With thanks to Shaul Shaked for showing me the text before it was published. For pub. info, see note on p. 254. The text is in Aramaic.

## "Shout"

For the relationship of crying to answering and to saving, see Isaiah 46:7, Psalms 9:13 and 107:6,28; and Job 19:7, 34:28, and 35:12.

*"like a man of war"*: An illuminating discussion of this passage can be found in Katheryn Pfisterer Darr, "Like Warrior, Like Woman: Destruction and Deliverance in Isaiah 42:10–17," *CBQ* 49 (1987):560–71.

## "Answer Me!"

For the communal liturgy, see *Megillat Ta'anit* 15a. Composed in the first century C.E., it was designed for communal fasts for the relief of drought. The midrashic passages quoted here are *Deuteronomy Rabbah* 2, 11, *Midrash Tehillim* 20:4, and *Midrash Tehillim* 20:2.

## "Aneni"

RAHAMANA: From the Slichot prayers first found in Geonic siddurim, including the Siddur of Rav. Saadiya Gaon.

M'AN D'ANE' LEHAYYATA: *Midrash Tehillim* 20:2.

MA'N DA'NEY LE'IMAK: *Midrash Tehillim* 20:4.

*"answering those in crisis"*: Psalm 20:1.

Jonah 2. I have chosen to include a man to remind us at this moment that the One who saves women also saves men. I chose Jonah because of the theme of being delivered from inside, which is like the delivery of the baby from inside the mother.

*"answering women in labor"*: *Deuteronomy Rabbah* 2, 11: *Midrash Tehilim* 20:4.

## The Oil of Birth

For contemporary practice, see Penny Armstrong and Sheryl Feldman, *A Wise Birth* (New York: Morrow, 1990).

The Mesopotamian story has survived in several versions. A Sumerian text was published by J. J. van Dijk, "Une Variante du thème de 'l'Esclave de la Lune,'" *Orientalia N.S.* 41(1972):339–48. A Middle Assyrian version was published by W. G. Lambert, "A Middle Assyrian Medical Text," *Iraq* 30 (1969):28–39. The Akkadian texts were edited and a composite suggested by W. Röllig, "Der Mondgott und die Kuh. Ein Lehrstück zur Problematik der Textüberlieferung im Alten Orient," *Orientalia N.S.* 54 (1985):260–73. Most recently Nick Veldhuis has analyzed the versions and motifs in *A Cow of Sîn* (Groningen: Styx Publications, 1991).

The two female spirits are identified in one version as *lamassus*, the protective deities; in another they are "daughters of Anu." The daughters of An are benevolent spirits who also appear in other incantations. But it is worth noting that the demon Lamashtu, the childsnatcher, is also the daughter of Anu.

Martin Stol, who translates the Neo-Assyrian text into Dutch in *Zwangerschap en geboorte bij de Babyloniers en in de Bijbel* (Leiden: 1983), suggested that the incantation was composed for Queen Geme-Sin's labor. We should note, however, that even if this is so, the durability of the incantation may also be attributed to the fact that it has even more power in Akkadian, where the sound similarity between *littu* ("cow") and *alittu*, ("the one who gives birth") would add a special significance to the use of the cow as the paradigm for the woman.

*"I wish I were there to do it"*: From a letter of Nettie McCormick to Anita McCormick Blain, the McCormick Papers, Wisconsin State Historical Society archives. This letter is quoted by Judith Leavitt, "Down to Death's Door: Women's Perceptions of Childbirth" in *Childbirth: The Beginning of Motherhood. Proceedings of the Second Motherhood Symposium*, ed. Sophie Colleau and Diane Roston (Madison: Women's Studies Research Center, University of Wisconsin, 1981), 113–30.

*Latter-day Saints' prayer*: This text is quoted by Maureen Ursenbach Beecher, "Birthing," in *Personal Voices: A Celebration of Dialogue*, ed. Mary Lythgoe Bradford (Salt Lake City: Signature Books, 1987) 143. She found the prayer penned into the minutes, 1901–1910, of the Oakley Second Ward Relief Society, Church Archives, Historical Department, the Church of Jesus Christ of Latter-Day Saints, Salt Lake City.

## "Sacred Place, Sacred Woman"

*"sacred to God through the ages"*: See Exodus 32:22–33.

## Oil for the One That Comes

*Cyrus as Messiah*: See Isaiah 45:1.
    *"two of oil"*: Zachariah 4:14.

*"the Spirit of the Lord"*: Isaiah 61:1, changing the "me" of the text to "you."

*"dare not kill"*: See 1 Samuel 26:9 and 2 Samuel 1:14 for David's admonition that the anointed are not to be touched. In 1 Samuel 26:16 David even declares that Abner is guilty because he failed to keep watch over the anointed. David is referring to the king of Israel, specifically Saul and—unspoken—himself. Today the words must be taken to refer to all people.

## "Sailing to Birth"

For editions of the Sumerian texts, see J. J. van Dijk, "Une Incantation accompagnant la naissance de l'homme," *Orientalia N.S.* 42(1973):502–7; idem, "Une Incantation accompagnant la naissance de l'homme," *Orientalia N.S.* 44 (1975):52–79; Mark Cohen, "Literary Texts from the Andrews University Archaeological Museum," *RA* 70 (1976):129–44; and G. Farber, "Another Old Babylonian Childbirth Incantation," *JNES* 43 (1984):311–16.

*"carnelian . . . lapis lazuli"*: It has been suggested that these refer to the sex of the baby. In any event, these minerals, like perfume and cedar wood, all came from the outermost regions of the known universe. The baby is coming from the other side of the world, the same realm to which humans return after death.

## At a Cesarean

*"We praise You, the Creator of lights"*: This is the blessing Jews recite over the candle that they light for the Havdalah ceremony, which marks the end of the Sabbath on Saturday evening.

*"who brings forth the bread from the earth"*: the standard Jewish blessing before eating bread.

*"not by means of an angel"*: This is the phrase that appears in the Passover Haggadah. Other occurrences are shorter, omitting the seraph. The haggadah continues:

> For I will go through the Land of Egypt,
> I and not an angel,
> and will smite all the firstborn,
> I and not a seraph,
> and against all the gods of Egypt I will execute judgments,
> I and not an agent,
> I the Lord, it is I and none other.

Then it provides a detailed commentary on Exodus 12:12 as proof of God's sole agency. In the midrashic compendium the *Mekhilta,* proof of the same idea is derived from Exodus 12:29: "Now it was the Lord who smote all the first born—not by means of an angel and not by means of a messenger."

*"rain for Israel"*: *Midrash Sifre Deuteronomy* 42 commenting on Deuteronomy 11:14.

*"Moses received the Torah"*: Avot de -Rabbi Natan B, p.2., giving as its textual proof Leviticus 26:46. For Moses' giving the people the Sabbath directly, see Rashi's comment on Exodus 31:12 and *Mekhilta* 3, 199.

*"we received them from Moses"*: For the references to Moses as mediator and for a scholarly discussion of his issue, see Judah Goldin, "Not by Means of an Angel and Not by Means of a Messenger," originally published as pp. 412–24 in *Religions in Antiquity: Essays in Memory of Erwin Ramsdell Goodenough*, Studies in the History of Religions 14, (Leiden: Brill, 1968). Now in Goldin, *Studies in Midrash and Related Literature*, JPS (Philadelphia, 1988): 163–73.

*"three partners in the birth"*: BT Niddah 31a.

## Deliverance

*"himlit"*: For delivery of a child, see Isaiah 66:7; in the context of deliverance of the people, see Isaiah 46:1–4.

*"let the one who is sealed up be released"*: This is a direct quotation from a Middle Assyrian medical text entitled "For a Woman in Childbirth," published by W.G. Lambert, "A Middle Assyrian Medical Text," *Iraq* 31(1969):29–39 q.v.

## "Come Forth!"

*"The way is open for you"*: From the incantation first published in *Orientalia* 42 and translated here on p. xxxi.

*"Christians have called to you"*: These Christian charms are collected by Forbes, *The Midwife and the Witch*, op.cit, 80–93. The instructions are included with the charms.

*"The great and awesome prayer"*: In the backs of some ancient prayer books, and copied also in Bela Yudita's, is a prayer for delivery which is attributed to the great mystical master Isaac Luria and which is called the "awesome prayer." This prayer provides that as labor goes on, this phrase be whispered into the ears of the woman.

In straits: For a ritual that connects the Red Sea crossing with birth, see the Passover ritual in Penina Adelman, *Miriam's Well: Rituals for Jewish Women around the Year* (New York: Biblio Press, 1986).

Blood: The many instances in which blood is used to purify the holy are assembled in the poem "Blood of the Covenant" on pp. 3–5.

*"in your blood, live"*: In Ezekiel 16, this is the sentence that God says as God sees the baby Jerusalem still covered in her birth blood. The Jewish tradition recites this sentence at the circumcision of baby boys.

# EPILOGUE

This is a version of the poem that is part of the covenant of creation, pp. 62–67.

# Acknowledgments

This has been a long and wonderful, daunting and arduous project. As time went on, documents got lost, pages, files, and my brain went blank, and it sometimes seemed that dark forces were intent on stopping me. But many people have helped and supported me during the sixteen years that I have worked on this project. I am deeply grateful to all of them, but I know that I cannot possibly acknowledge them all. Some names I will forget to mention, and I already regret omitting these people. And some names I never knew, names of people who heard me give readings of parts of this work and came up to me with tears, words of encouragement and moving stories of their own or their wives' experiences. I would like to thank all of them, who have been the forces of light that sustained me. Above all, I single out:

My personal support system:

Allan Kensky, my husband, who was initially skeptical but always encouraging, and kept me intellectually honest with his refusal to let me make careless or unsupported statements. He is uneasy with the symbolism of angels, but he is certainly my personal angel.

Penny Gill, long-standing friend and soulmate, who logged many hours of telephone encouragement.

The faculty and students at the Reconstructionist Rabbinical College of Wyncote, Pennsylvania, who provided a creative and spiritual community of support and interest during the last eight years.

And my children, Meira and Eitan Kensky, who sometimes had to endure the sleepy presence of a mother who wrote much of this book in the "holy hours" between midnight and three in the morning.


My technical support system:

Wendy Gabay, the associate librarian at the Reconstructionist Rabbinical College and, earlier, Judith Leifer, the librarian at the Penn Judaica Center. Without their labors at inter-library loan, it would have been impossible to work on so far-ranging a project.

Nathelda McGee and Marsha Peeler, secretaries at the University of Chicago Divinity School, who endured with grace the many printouts and mailings of the final phase of this work.


And my professional colleagues who selflessly shared their work-in-progress:

Walter Farber, Sumerologist at the Oriental Institute of Chicago, whom I visited several times to consult on Lamashtu, and who was generous with both his time and his provisional manuscript.

Chava Weissler, Professor of Religion at Lehigh University and expert on *tekhines*, who gave me Xeroxes of the childbirth *tekhines* to study, and years later, after I had learned to read and translate them, took the time to meet with me for technical information.

Nina Beth Cardin, Rabbi and editor of *Sh'ma* magazine, who gave me a Xerox of the JTS manuscript of Bela Yudita's prayer book years before she published her edition in *Out of the Depths I Call to You.*

Shaul Shaked, who gave a stranger who walked into his office unpublished manuscripts of Cairo Genizah manuscript texts.

And Virginia Rendburg, whom I have never met, who responded to a telephone call seeking further information about St. Marguerite by sending me a chapter from her unfinished manuscript on medieval popular piety.

The willingness of these colleagues to share their information and insights is what scholarship is all about.

# INDEX

TIKVA FRYMER-KENSKY is Professor of Hebrew Bible at the University of Chicago Divinity School and the Director of Biblical Studies for the Reconstructionist Rabbinical College in Philadephia. She divides her time between Philadelphia and Chicago.

A 1965 graduate of City College with a B.H.L. from the Jewish Theological Seminary, she received her Ph.D. in Assyriology and Sumerology from Yale University in 1977. She has received grants from the Annenberg Foundation, the NEH, and the ACLS, and she has also been awarded fellowships from the Danforth Foundation and the Woodrow Wilson Foundation. She has taught at the Jewish Theological Seminary, University of Michigan, and Wayne State. Author of *In the Wake of the Goddesses*, she has written over one hundred articles and academic papers, and lectures widely to both scholarly and general audiences.